The Sixth Column

OTHER BOOKS BY ROGER BURLINGAME:

Don't Let Them Scare You
Peace Veterans
March of the Iron Men
Engines of Democracy
Whittling Boy: The Story of Eli Whitney
Of Making Many Books
Machines That Built America
Backgrounds of Power
General Billy Mitchell
Henry Ford
Benjamin Franklin: The First Mr. American
The American Conscience
I Have Known Many Worlds
Scientists behind the Inventors
(With Alden Stevens) Victory without Peace

THE SIXTH COLUMN

by Roger Burlingame

"*Nothing that the agents of communism have done or can do in this country is so dangerous to the United States as what they have induced us . . . to do to ourselves.*"
—Alan Barth

J. B. Lippincott Company
Philadelphia and New York

To the memory of ELMER DAVIS
who reminded us that we were born free

Preface

THE IMPULSE that prompted this book came during the preparation of my recent biography of Elmer Davis, the news commentator who insisted that we were born free and were being frightened out of our birthright. The title of my biography—*Don't Let Them Scare You*—was taken from one of Davis's speeches and was his constant warning to confused Americans.

Davis's voice ceased in the midst of the McCarthy era. It had restored many of us to reason and sanity. Its echo is still with us, and although the panic of McCarthyism has temporarily subsided, the danger that Davis warned against is perennially present.

It seemed to me then that there was more to be said. Davis would have said it had he lived. I felt this when I wrote about him, and I felt, too, a kind of obligation to pursue his inquiry into the reasons for the subversion of which he was so acutely aware —a subversion more insidious and more dangerous than any the Communists have yet devised.

It was communism, to be sure, that had scared the men that were trying to scare us; but communism had also provided American demagogues with a means of political power. Indirectly, then, communism had weakened us. But its unwitting instruments were these very instigators of panic. This is a fact of which the Russians are now aware. They know now that the self-styled anti-Communists who spread fear and suspicion among our people, who turn friends and neighbors against each other, who promote police-state methods as a substitute for judicial process, and who attempt to suppress free speech and free assembly are communism's strongest allies. If we are to conduct a realistic fight against communism, we would do well to begin by combating these Americans who, without knowing it, are giving aid and comfort to our true enemy.

Are these men and women, these groups and organizations traitors and bands of traitors? Do they compose what the late Ernest Hemingway made notorious as the "Fifth Column"? Not quite. They are more elusive. Marching as they do under a banner of patriotism, they are more difficult to detect and to thwart.

For them, therefore, I have devised the term Sixth Column. In order that we may know its true nature and the extent of its destructive power, I have attempted to present a history of the Sixth Column from its inception immediately after the Bolshevik revolution in Russia. I have tried, too, to appraise its present and future potential.

In the United States, the seasons of fear or hysteria engendered by the Sixth Column have come in cycles. The first, during the chaos following the first World War, was the most violent and the least rational. The next, on the eve of the New Deal, was a corollary of the Depression, when, in many quarters, there was the expectation of actual revolution. From 1938 to 1942, to the accompaniment of the Stalin-Hitler pact and the Russian attack on Finland, a Red scare was nurtured by the Dies Committee, predecessor of the standing Un-American Activities Committee of the House of Representatives. Soon after World War II, in which the Soviet Union was our military ally, investigating committees in the Senate took on judicial functions in pursuit of alleged disloyal Americans who had "sold China down the river to the Communists." Concern about the Far Eastern situation was, of course, stimulated by the Korean war. This was followed by the McCarthy era in which occurred the most hysterical witch hunts since 1920. Finally, the Sixth Column began its march under the banner of "conservatism" or the Right wing. Leading the parade is the John Birch Society, repudiated even by conservative Senator Barry Goldwater, veteran House Un-American Activities Committee member Richard Nixon, and William F. Buckley's conservative *National Review*. Other right-wing organizations, such as the "Minutemen," go even deeper into the lunatic fringe; all are open to ridicule, and ridicule may defeat them.

At the bottom of each cycle, there is a temporary return to sanity and, usually, a rejection of erstwhile heroes who have been exposed as demagogues. Sometimes this results from a change of focus when we become aware of a more immediate menace than communism, as, for example, when we saw the fascist threat. But the old scare has always come back because it has always been profitable to the Sixth Column operators.

We are probably, at this moment of writing, approaching the bottom of a cycle. There is a strong reaction from the American practice of anti-communism. This reaction has been brought about by the extremists. Their antagonism is not only to communism but to much of the traditional American way of life. Today, they even reject democracy itself. To good Americans this is intolerable. It makes us wonder how much damage has been done to our ideals and our freedoms by the organizations and programs that preceded and paved the way for the extremists: Congressional investigating committees, loyalty boards, censors of print and speech, Americanism committees in patriotic societies, book burners, and Justice Department staffs.

This book attempts to estimate that damage. In telling of the immense hurt that has been done in the past not only to our democratic faith and to our most cherished institutions but to hundreds of innocent American citizens, it presents a warning for the future.

For the Sixth Column is not dead. It will march again and again in new forms, new disguises. Those of us who love our country, who have faith in our particular kind of democracy, who accept the definitions of the rights and the dignity of man that our Founding Fathers gave us, must be ready for it.

Acknowledgments

I HAVE ACKNOWLEDGED all published source material in footnotes and listed in a bibliography such documents, books, and articles as I have cited in the text as well as those which have provided me with background reading. I am indebted to Attorney General Stanley Mosk of California for a copy of the report on the John Birch Society which he and Assistant Attorney General Howard H. Jewel prepared for Governor of California Edmund G. Brown. I also thank Mr. Will Maslow of the American Jewish Congress for a report entitled "The Radical Right: Fact Sheet."

My thanks to Ernest Angell, Chairman of the Board of the American Civil Liberties Union, and to Director Marie M. Runyon for a quantity of valuable material prepared by the Union. My old friend David Mearns of the Library of Congress, who has helped me in all my work over the last quarter century, came again to my assistance in making special facilities of that world's greatest library available to me. I am grateful to the librarians of the New York Public Library who have dug out many government documents and the microfilms of old newspapers for my examination; especially to Miss Shirley Dakin of the economics division, who has given me much patient assistance.

For useful occasional help in various phases of the work, I thank my friends Stuart Chase, Ordway Tead, Arthur Sweetser, and Armitage Watkins; and for special assistance, I thank Mr. William Winter of the American Broadcasting Company in San Francisco.

The book and article material on which I have leaned most

11

heavily is that written by Mr. Alan Barth of the *Washington Post*. No one, I believe, has interpreted the infringement of our liberties and the subversion of our Constitution in the interests of so-called antiradical movements with greater wisdom and clarity than Mr. Barth. *Government by Investigation* and *The Loyalty of Free Men* are true masterpieces in the field. I want also to thank Mr. Denver Lindley of Viking Press for making the possession of these books easy for me.

I have had constant recourse to Professor Carr's monumental history of the *House Un-American Activities Committee, 1945– 1950*. These were the most critical years in the life of that committee, and Professor Carr's study deals with them with fairness and attention to detail.

As always, I have had not only the most meticulous but also the kindest and most considerate editing from my publisher's managing editor, George Stevens; working with him has been uninterrupted pleasure. I thank also Miss Isabelle Holland of Lippincott for her assistance, and I owe my usual indebtedness to my "author's representative," Kenneth Littauer.

My wife has been constantly on deck as she has always been.

For patient and extremely accurate work on the manuscript, bibliography, and index, I thank Mrs. Christine G. Loring, now Mrs. Rodman Valentine.

Contents

I. Climate of Fear, 1919–1920

SINCE ITS FIRST ESTABLISHMENT following the revolution of October, 1917,[1] the Union of Soviet Socialist Republics has followed a course calculated to alarm the peoples of the western nations. From the start, it appeared to pose a threat to the capitalist economy, notably the system of free enterprise which had built the industrial powers of Britain and the United States and of most of the nations of western Europe. The success of the Bolshevik revolution in Russia and the avowed purpose of the victorious Russian Bolshevik party to bring about world revolution were profoundly disturbing to those societies in which there had been inadequate adjustment of the conflicts between labor and management or a failure to lessen the distance between the extremes of rich and poor.

Though Great Britain and the United States lived, for the most part, in freedom from the social conditions which, for centuries, had plagued Russia and which continued to harass parts of Europe, there has been, nevertheless, even in the sturdy Anglo-Saxon democracies, a constant fear of the Communist menace.

The first acute symptoms of that fear appeared in the United States in the year following the Armistice of 1918. The withdrawal of Russia from the war and the Treaty of Brest-Litovsk, giving huge advantages to Germany, had produced a profound shock in all the Allied nations. The Allies in that time seemed

[1] October on the Russian calendar, November on ours. George F. Kennan, *Russia and the West under Lenin and Stalin,* Boston: Little, Brown & Co., 1961, pp. 11, 12.

17

to be facing defeat. Their only hope lay in the entrance of the United States, which took place in April, 1917. Yet before the Americans could arrive in any effective force, the collapse of Russia made it possible for the Germans to withdraw their forces from the eastern front and face the new ally with redoubled strength. From the moment, then, of the October revolution, a wave of bitterness spread through the American people which was to culminate in national hysteria.

And there were other factors. The Armistice was followed, in the United States, by widespread labor unrest and the strikes that were a prelude to the new labor organization of the succeeding years. Returning soldiers in the spring of 1919 were exceedingly resentful of these agitations that beclouded the dawn of what many thought was the millennium after Armageddon. These workers, they said, had lived in peace and on the fat of the land, earning enormous wages, while the soldiers were sleeping in mud under fire and living through every kind of discomfort and suffering with the private's meager pay of thirty dollars a month. It was natural, then, for the veterans, their families, and their sympathizers to turn against the workers. Furthermore, the Russian affair had given them a convenient label to pin on the American agitator. Probably, he was a Bolshevik-American counterpart of the Russian revolutionary who had brought about the Russian treachery. From this point it was easy to progress to the cloak-and-dagger fiction that there was a vast conspiracy directed from Moscow to overthrow the government of the United States "by force and violence." The American Bolsheviks, it came to be said, were already organized in countless "cells" distributed throughout the country, ready to rise, at a given signal, against all constituted authority.

Such a picture was appealing to the American romantic mind. It suggested the free-for-all conflicts of the frontier days when vigilantes took the law into their own hands and shot the horse thieves, cattle rustlers, and claim jumpers who obstructed the continental conquest by the advancing pioneers. Unless, now, the forces of law and order could immediately scotch the plot

18

and rid the country of the Bolshevik vermin, these angry soldiers, accustomed to a climate of killing, would also take things into their own hands and do the "mopping up" job themselves.

The mood of the home-coming "boys" was aggravated by civilian fears. Industrialists who had made fortunes during the war apparently faced the possibility that their gains would be taken from them by the socialist government which would follow the success of the conspiracy. These tycoons drew into their camp many an honest and patriotic company owner or corporation executive who had conscientiously spent the war years in helping the war effort, but who was now faced with the labor unrest which would prevent him, in the peace, from getting "back to normal."

In 1919, too, American soldiers came back from their campaign in Russia where they had gone with an Allied contingent to fight the Bolsheviks.[2] Their experiences in the abortive attempt in the winter cold at Archangel hardly inclined them toward sympathy with the new Russia. And they had tales to tell of post-revolutionary brutalities, of the bloody liquidation of the Russian bourgeoisie; rumors of naked human carcasses hanging in the butcher shops—stories which, true, false, or patently absurd, the American public was only too ready to believe. Further, businessmen impressed the soldiers with the notion that it was a soldier's duty—in addition to saving their country from the Germans—to save it from Bolshevism as well.

What the American people at large did not, and could not, know was the extreme weakness of the infant Soviet regime; the immense losses of men and money that Russia had suffered in the war; the difficulties that beset Lenin and Trotsky in their efforts to bring the recalcitrant "republics" into line; the frustration which was meeting the attempts to unify the vast, sprawling territory into a single nation; the great economic concessions the Soviet Socialists would have to make before the new economy could become successful or of Lenin's postponement of the

[2] Kennan, *op. cit.*, chap. 5.

Marxian world revolution until such time as he could consolidate his gains and compensate his losses within Russia.[3]

Nor could the American public at large know of the conditions behind the domestic labor unrest. We have since learned of the persecution of the loggers' unions in the great timber country of the Pacific Northwest with its series of bloody raids on union halls and union meetings; of the savage acts of sadistic strikebreakers bent on frustrating labor organizations; of the feudal oppression of company towns in industrial areas—communities in which every business and all property was company-owned—in which, however, workers were forced to live; of the motives behind such hated organizations as the Industrial Workers of the World and of the struggle of workers to live under the burdens of post-war inflation.

It was not unnatural that, in ignorance of all these things, the people should have thought and behaved as they did. But that the presumably sane, stable, and knowledgeable government of the United States should have abetted this ignorance, enhanced the mounting hysteria and responded to the irresponsible demands of frightened citizens with acts of pure panic has marked this era as almost the nadir of national morale.[4]

It was in this feverish milieu that the American Sixth Column, as we know it today, was born. It is true that throughout our history there have been sporadic betrayals of American ideals by persons who did not know they were traitors. But the Sixth Column which had its birth in 1919, has had a steady growth; from that point on, its power has been increasingly accelerated.

2

The first tocsin was sounded in the Senate. Not more than three months after the Armistice of November, 1918, mass meet-

[3] John W. Wheeler-Bennett, *The Forgotten Peace: Brest-Litovsk, March 1918,* New York: William Morrow & Co., 1939, p. 147.

[4] Robert K. Murray, *Red Scare: A Study in National Hysteria, 1919–1920,* Minneapolis: University of Minnesota Press, 1955, *passim.* This book gives a detailed history with abundant documentation of the period.

20

ings were held in Washington supporting the Soviet armed forces in their attempt to bring all Russia into the Soviet Union. These armies were, at that very moment, being opposed by Allied troops including Americans. This seemed to senators to be as close to giving aid and comfort to the enemy as possible at such a distance.

As usual in such crises, the cry went up, "Investigate!" Conveniently there was actually an investigating subcommittee at work; it was, however, engaged in the ex post facto business of inquiring into "the brewing industry and German propaganda." When the Senate ordered this subcommittee of the Judiciary Committee to turn from its stale pursuit to the sensational Bolshevist bogey, its members must have been delighted. It was now told to

cover any efforts being made to propagate in this country the principles of any party exercising or claiming to exercise authority in Russia, whether such efforts originate in this country or are incited or financed from abroad, and, further, to inquire into any effort to incite the overthrow of the Government of this country, or all government, by force, or by the destruction of life or property or the general cessation of industry.[5]

After this suggestion that such overthrow was possible—an odd position for the upper chamber of the United States Congress—the subcommittee under the chairmanship of North Carolina's Senator Lee S. Overman got down to business. The Senate, still, in those days, under the impression that congressional investigating committees were instituted to find a basis for new legislation and not, as later evolved, to become exposing and punitive bodies, resolved to consult with the Department of Justice.[6] The Attorney General, T. W. Gregory, who already knew about the subversive rallies, suggested that he had no evidence that government overthrow had been advocated by their speak-

[5] Senate Resolution 439 57 CR 2654 (Feb. 4, 1919).
[6] 57 CR 2654 SR 437 (Feb. 4, 1919).

ers and would like to have any that the subcommittee found.[7]
Overman then held seventeen hearings and produced no such
evidence.

Nevertheless, the subcommittee's communication with Attorney General Gregory put him on the alert. Alexander Mitchell
Palmer, who was appointed Attorney General soon afterward,
may have seen an opportunity for some highly favorable publicity and having become, from modest beginnings, a highly
ambitious official, kept his ears open for any demands from the
citizens that he act on his own to oppose the terrifying movement. As the press had taken advantage of the rallies to exploit
the menace, the demands soon came and, according to the Attorney General, could not be ignored.

Palmer's career up to that point had not been wholly consistent. He had been born into an old Quaker family and had continued in that faith through his education at a Moravian
parochial school and at Swarthmore College from which he had
graduated *summa cum laude*. He then studied law and was
admitted to the Pennsylvania bar. During his subsequent practice, he became interested in local politics in his native town of
Stroudsburg and, in 1908, he was elected Democratic Representative from his district.

In Congress, he was known as an insurgent and a reformer,
a strong advocate in 1910 and 1912 of such progressive measures
as the anti-child labor law. In 1912, he played an active part in
the nomination of Woodrow Wilson and in Wilson's election. He
was rewarded by an offer of the position of Secretary of War;
he declined on the grounds of his membership in the Society of
Friends. When war came, however, he accepted the office of
Alien Property Custodian. His management of this post was
severely criticized on grounds of personal favoritism; this did not,
however, prevent his appointment as Attorney General in March,
1919.[8]

[7] 57 CR 3247 (Feb. 13, 1919).
[8] Robert K. Murray, "Alexander Mitchell Palmer," in *Dictionary of American Biography*, New York: Charles Scribner's Sons, 1928–1958, XXII,
Supplement Two, p. 510.

At this point, Palmer seems to have become a changed man. Whether he was dominated by a growing, an almost pathological, ambition, or was genuinely roused to frenzy by what he fancied was an imminent threat to his government, his action was anything but liberal and peaceable. In his first year as Attorney General, he betrayed both his religion and his political convictions. One is tempted to believe that had not the President in that time been so preoccupied with the peace treaty and the League of Nations, and later been paralyzed by a nervous breakdown, he would have removed Palmer from the office that he degraded.

As head of the Department of Justice, Palmer's first moves were against labor. Because a treaty of peace had not yet been signed with Germany, he took advantage of the wartime Lever Act[9]—prohibiting restriction of fuel production for the war's duration—to obtain an injunction against a coal strike. Since the Bolshevik label had already been applied by public opinion to the miners, Palmer's act had the support of most of the press. Following this by a direct move against members of the American Communist Party, he used another wartime statute—the Act of October 16, 1918, as amended, which permitted the Secretary of Labor to deport aliens who were connected with organizations believing in or advocating the overthrow of government by unconstitutional means. Co-operating with the Department of Labor, the Attorney General conducted raids to round up Communist aliens and, in December, 1919, after wholesale arrests, deported 249 of them to Russia. This performance was given wide publicity and greatly enhanced the climate of fear throughout the nation.[1]

The first deportation came in December, 1919, on the steamship *Buford*, nicknamed the "Soviet Ark." For this, men had been arrested at meetings in various parts of the country, sometimes without warrant or other considerations of their legal rights. An article in *The Survey* in January, 1920, tells of their plight:

[9] Aug. 10, 1917. House Doc. 837; 65:2.
[1] "The Deportations" in *The Survey*, Feb. 22, 1919, p. 722.

The wives of the *Buford* deportees hoped up to the last moment to accompany their husbands. Had they been allowed to do so, and had they been given a few days to attend to personal affairs, the subsequent tragedy would have been averted. As it was, they were not even told definitely when their husbands would sail. The first knowledge many of them had of this sailing was the announcement in the newspapers next morning. Thus, they not only were not allowed to say goodbye but had no opportunity for delivering trunks, suit cases, outfits of clothing, food and other personal necessaries which they had prepared in the event of deportation.[2]

Other men who were not deported were held in jail for as much as five months, during which they received brutal treatment, only to be released later without trial. In one case when there was an evident miscarriage of justice, the victim later told his story in an affidavit published after his release.

In the autumn of 1919 [Simeon Nakhwat testified under oath] I was a member of the Union of Russian workers. I am not an anarchist, Socialist or Bolshevik, and do not take much interest in political theories. I joined the Russian workers because I was a workman speaking Russian and wanted to associate with other Russians and have the benefit of the social intercourse and instruction in mechanics which the society gave. By trade I am a machinist.

On November 8, 1919, I was at a meeting of Russians in Bridgeport, who had come together to discuss ways and means for buying an automobile for instruction purposes . . . I was arrested with all the other men at the meeting, 63 in number. . . . No warrant of arrest was shown me then or at any other time, nor did I see any warrant shown to anyone else who was arrested. . . . I was held in the Hartford jail for six weeks without any hearing. . . .[3]

[2] Winthrop D. Lane, "The Buford Widows" in *The Survey*, Jan. 10, 1920, pp. 391–92.

[3] *Report upon the Illegal Practices of the U.S. Department of Justice* (hereafter referred to as *Illegal Practices Report*), Washington: National Popular Government League, 1920, Exhibit 1a.

After he had been confined for six weeks, the agent who had originally arrested Nakhwat came to his cell and asked some questions which he was unable to answer. This federal policeman then

> struck me twice with his fist . . . whereupon I fell. He then kicked me and I became unconscious.

Later, because of an infection in his hand, the prisoner asked for a doctor. When he repeated his request, he was put in solitary confinement in

> a room in the basement of the jail with a cement floor, cement walls and an iron door. The room was pitch dark. . . . The floor of the room was hot and the walls were very warm to the touch. I stayed in this room for thirty-six hours.

During that time he was given a slice of bread and a drink of water. He was released from the Hartford jail on April 7, after five months of imprisonment.[4]

A man named Peter Musek was put in the Hartford jail because he went there to see a friend who was a prisoner on a similar reckless charge. He was held there from the day before Christmas, 1919, till March 20, 1920, when he was released on bail. Meanwhile, he had been frequently beaten, threatened with hanging if he did not answer questions about his friends, and told that he would be put in a gas chamber and suffocated if he remained silent. While he was confined, he had his books and watch stolen, presumably by guards or federal agents.[5]

In November, 1919, a barber, Anton Dimitroff, was arrested while shaving a customer and was forced to quit the shop (which he owned) leaving the customer half shaved. He was kept in a cell from November 12, 1919, to April 7, 1920, when he was released on bail. He was forced to sell his shop with its entire

[4] *Ibid.*
[5] *Ibid.*, Exhibit 1b.

25

equipment at a loss. He was without means of buying new tools and, from his confinement and beatings, in bad health.[6]

In his affidavit, Alexander Bukowetsky, whose wife and child were beaten by guards when they came to visit him, testified:

> When I came to America I came with the thought that I was coming to a free country,—a place of freedom and happiness, and I was anxious to come—to get away from the Czaristic form of Government. As much as I was anxious to come here to America, I am a hundred times more anxious to run away from Americanism to return to Soviet Russia, where at least I will be able to live.
>
> For six months I have been confined in jail, the Government refusing to either deport or release me together with my wife and children. They have been left, during this time without means of support . . .
>
> The Government has decided that we are to be deported. We ask only that this sentence be carried out that we with our families be deported to Soviet Russia, and that this cruel and inhuman policy of keeping men for six months in jail under sentence of deportation, refusing to either deport or release us, and leaving our families to starve, be ended.[7]

It is not on record how many Communists were thus manufactured by the United States Department of Justice out of Russians who had left Russia before the October revolution of 1917. Nor is it on record what stories these deportees told on their return to a Russia which had become Communist. It is possible that such gossip contributed to the general "ignorance" of the United States that has prevailed among the Soviet people since 1920.

The affidavits from which these quotations are made were included among many others in a report signed by twelve American lawyers and published in May, 1920, by the National Popular

[6] *Ibid.*, Exhibit 1c.
[7] *Ibid.*, Exhibit 5a.

Government League in Washington.[8] The authors, who conducted an intensive investigation of conditions in the autumn and winter of 1919-1920, were:

R. G. Brown, of Memphis, Tennessee; Zechariah Chafee, Jr., Felix Frankfurter and Roscoe Pound of Cambridge, Massachusetts; Ernest Freund of Chicago; Swinburne Hale and Frank R. Walsh of New York City; Francis Fisher Kane and David Wallerstein of Philadelphia; Alfred S. Niles of Baltimore; Jackson C. Ralston of Washington; Tyrrall Williams of St. Louis.

In the preamble to this report the authors stated:

To the American People:

For more than six months we, the undersigned lawyers, whose sworn duty it is to uphold the Constitution and Laws of the United States, have seen with growing apprehension the continued violation of that Constitution and breaking of these Laws by the Department of Justice of the United States.[9]

3

The arrests and deportations of 1919 were, however, only the beginning of the Attorney General's campaign. What has since become notorious as the "Red Scare" first showed its truly sensational aspect on the day after New Year's, 1920.

Indeed, beneath the smoke, there was fire. In several parts of the country there had been sporadic bomb plots and bomb explosions during the first post-war year. In April, 1919, a bomb had been found in the mail of Ole Hansen, mayor of Seattle, Washington, the scene of an intensive Red pursuit. Immediately afterward the maid of Senator Thomas R. Hardwick of Georgia, who had voted for the restriction of immigration, had her hands blown off when she opened a package addressed to the Senator. Sixteen packages addressed to prominent men were found, in the New York City Post Office, to contain bombs. The lack of method and indiscriminate targets of the plots were shown by the fact

[8] *Illegal Practices Report.*
[9] *Ibid.*, p. 3.

that Postmaster General Burleson, Supreme Court Justice Oliver Wendell Holmes, and Federal Judge Landis were among those threatened. In evident retaliation for the acts just noted, the Washington home of the Attorney General himself was wrecked by a bomb explosion on June 1, 1919—an incident which may have enhanced his zeal.[1]

Undoubtedly among the conspirators there were some newly converted Communists—workers who had joined the American branch of the Communist Party, established soon after the Armistice. Undoubtedly there were also some of the crackpots we have always with us, who had been inflamed by the prevailing hysteria and by the hyperbolic statements of men in public life. That the conspiracies were directed from Moscow may be doubted. The Soviet government was too busy, at the time, with internal frustrations to take part in such remote exercises.

Be that as it may, the national scare was not without cause. The mood of the people was not calm. The emotional excitement caused by the end of the war, the return of the soldiers to their homes and the restlessness and often the neuroses of the soldiers themselves did not provide an ideal medium for the return of "normalcy." At the same time, the people were sharply divided between those who favored American participation in the League of Nations and those who identified normalcy with isolationism. It was, then, an appropriate time for government to exercise a quieting influence and to attempt to bring order out of a natural post-war chaos as a prelude to a decade of business as usual.

Instead, the government, deprived of its president, not only failed to exert restraint on the hysteria but did everything possible to increase it. The Attorney General, having learned or suspected that the two Communist parties that had mushroomed since November—the Communist Party and the Communist Labor Party—planned to hold meetings on the second of January, in cities all over the country, saw good fishing ahead.

Through secret agents he uncovered some definite plans for

[1] Oscar T. Barck, Jr., and Nelson M. Blake, *Since 1900: A History of the United States in Our Times*, New York: The Macmillan Co., 1947, p. 275.

meetings. In other groups no meetings were scheduled. The Department of Justice, therefore, decided to arrange them. Its Bureau of Investigation (later, the FBI) planted undercover *agents provocateurs* in the suspicious groups who, disguised as members, were to agitate for meetings to be held on the evening of January 2.

> Agents of the Department of Justice [stated the lawyers' report] have been introduced into radical organizations for the purpose of informing upon their members or inciting them to activities; these agents have even been instructed from Washington to arrange meetings upon certain dates for the express object of facilitating wholesale raids and arrests.[2]

Meanwhile the Attorney General had secured from the Department of Labor some three thousand deportation warrants, many of which were to be filled in with the suspect's name after his arrest. So on the scheduled night, the simultaneous raids took place in communities from coast to coast, on meetings some of which later turned out not to have been for purposes of radical agitation but were innocent gatherings of persons in similar trades.

About four thousand persons were taken in, including American citizens, college graduates, skilled mechanics, and boys still in short trousers. The raiders seized everyone on the premises whether they were radical agitators, mere curiosity seekers, or persons who had drifted in to the meetings by accident or to get out of the cold.

A well-documented account of these raids is given in Robert K. Murray's *Red Scare.*

> On January 2, more than 4000 suspected radicals were rounded up in thirty-three major cities, covering twenty-three states. . . . Often such arrests were made without the formality of warrants as bureau agents entered bowling alleys, pool halls,

[2] *Illegal Practices Report*, p. 3.

cafes, club rooms and even homes and seized everyone in sight. Families were separated; prisoners were held incommunicado and deprived of their right to legal counsel. . . .

In the New England area . . . about 800 persons were seized of whom approximately half were taken to the immigrant station in Boston and then shipped to Deer Island in Boston Harbor. In the shifting process, the prisoners were forced to march in chains from the immigrant station to the dock. . . . Upon arriving at Deer Island the prisoners found conditions deplorable; heat was lacking, sanitation was poor. . . . One captive plunged five stories to his death, another went insane and two others died of pneumonia. The remaining half of the 800 who were not sent to Deer Island were released after two or three days when it was determined they were in no way connected with the radical movement. For example, thirty-nine bakers in Lynn, Massachusetts . . . were released when it was learned that they had come together . . . for the inoffensive purpose of establishing a cooperative bakery. . . .

In the Detroit raid about 800 persons were arrested and imprisoned from three to six days in a dark, windowless, narrow corridor in the city's antiquated Federal Building. The prisoners were forced to sleep on the bare floor and stand in long lines for access to the solitary toilet. Some, unable to wait, were forced to urinate in the corridor itself, and, as the custodian later testified, "Before many days . . . the stench was quite unbearable."[3]

On the sixth day after the arrests, eight hundred of the prisoners were released when it was discovered that they had no interest whatever in the radical movement.

Meanwhile, the people, being fed through the press that was streaming from Palmer's office—much of it in "boiler plate" form, luridly illustrated—could hardly be blamed for believing in the existence of a huge Bolshevist plot. College students, always inflammable, agitated against their teachers and many an

[3] Murray, *Red Scare*, pp. 213, 215. Frederick R. Barkeley, "Jailing Radicals in Detroit" in *The Nation*, Jan. 31, 1920, p. 137.

innocent professor was persecuted, sometimes deprived of his job.

An English journalist, quoted by A. G. Gardiner in *Portraits and Portents* (1926), said:

No one who was in the United States, as I chanced to be, in the autumn of 1919, will forget the feverish condition of the public mind at that time. It was hagridden by the spectre of Bolshevism. . . . Property was in an agony of fear, and the horrid name, 'Radical' covered the most innocent departure from conventional thought with a suspicion of desperate purpose.[4]

4

At the peak of the national hysteria, the New York State legislature got in on the act. It created a so-called legislative investigation committee headed by State Senator Clayton Lusk, a lawyer from Cortland, N.Y.[5] This was a sort of prototype of later federal committees of investigation in that it soon abandoned its purpose of finding bases for new state laws and became a punitive agency. Indeed in its first public statement of its objectives, the chairman asked for "the full cooperation of the state and city police . . . and of the Federal investigating bureaus."

In the spring and early summer of 1919, the committee, aided by the city police, led raids on the Russian Soviet Bureau, the Rand School of Social Science, and the headquarters of the left-wing Socialists in New York City, arrested many persons, destroyed much property, and captured tons of alleged Bolshevist propaganda. In November the committee conducted raids on some seventy alleged "Red Centers" in the city, and took more than a thousand persons into custody. In explanation of the committee's acts, Chairman Lusk said:

[4] Alfred George Gardiner, *Portraits and Portents,* New York: Harper and Brothers, 1926, p. 13.
[5] Report of the Joint Legislative Committee of the State of New York Investigating Seditious Activities, 1920.

These organizations are a direct public challenge to the authorities of the State and nation. . . . It seems to me that the time has come to put into force stern measures to do away with this agitation and punish these disloyal leaders in the movement.[6]

"Mr. Lusk," comments Lawrence H. Chamberlain in his book *Loyalty and Legislative Action,* "was not speaking as one recommending new legislation but as an adjunct of the executive machinery."[7]

As the main performance of the Lusk Committee was concerned with the instruction and curricula of the New York schools, we shall examine further into its activities in a chapter on the work of the Sixth Column in the restriction of education.

Late in 1919, the New York State Assembly expelled five of its duly elected members because they were members of the Socialist Party, the argument being that a Socialist could not support the Constitution.

This is not, [commented Chief Justice Charles Evans Hughes] in my judgment, American government . . . I count it a most serious mistake to proceed, not against individuals charged with violation of law, but against masses of our citizens combined for political action, by denying them . . . action by the ballot box and through duly elected representatives in legislative bodies.[8]

All of these things were in the pattern of dictatorship, not of democracy. That this kind of subversion should be encouraged by government makes it wholly authoritarian. Many of the practices almost precisely paralleled those carried out then and later

[6] *New York Times,* Nov. 9, 1919, p. 1.
[7] This book by the Dean of Columbia College gives a detailed report on the entire conduct of the Lusk Committee. Ithaca, N.Y.: Cornell University Press, 1951, p. 16.
[8] Barck and Blake, *op. cit.,* p. 278.

in the Soviet régime. In other words, the American Sixth Column in what it supposed was a patriotic effort was meticulously following the Party Line.

5

In the midst of the confusion, the soldiers brought back with them from the A.E.F. in Europe the embryo of a super-patriotic organization which would one day be a formidable bulwark of the Sixth Column. This had emerged from a meeting in Paris and was one of the phenomena which, in the United States, always follow a war and carry on the curious nostalgia for combat in veteran soldiers. It was called the American Legion; it started with high, if somewhat inflated, ideals and later became dedicated to two things: money reward and the eagle's scream. Through the years, when it has not been bringing pressure on the Congress to pay for past patriotism, it has been trying to revive the raucous braggadocio of frontier days when our adolescent country, safe behind its splendid isolation, was indeed, as Kipling said, "the scandal of the elder earth."

In its first year, 1919, the Legion distinguished itself by a demonstration against a union hall in Centralia, Washington. The hall was used by a local of a "loggers' " organization affiliated with the I.W.W. In the ensuing panic, several Legionnaires were shot. This event, described by the Legion as a "massacre," was followed by one of the most brutal lynchings in American history; for it Legionnaires got the credit. One of the men who had done the shooting was dragged from the jail in which he had been placed after arrest, then was castrated and hanged from a bridge. The lynching followed an Armistice Day parade in which the Legion marched in uniform. The Legionnaires in cahoots with the businessmen of Centralia led the attack.[9]

[9] Ralph Chaplin, *The Centralia Conspiracy*, Chicago: Thos. Whitehead, 1924. Robert K. Murray, *Red Scare*, pp. 181–89. Arthur G. Hays, *Trial by Prejudice*, New York: Covici, Friede, 1935, pp. 254–60. 115 Washington Reports 409–28. Robert L. Tyler, "Violence at Centralia, 1919," in *Pacific Northwest Quarterly*, vol. 45, no. 3 (July, 1954)—an article that gives abundant source material.

In the mad decade of the twenties when the capital stank with the corruption brought in by President Harding's so-called Ohio gang, when the rumrunners and hijackers of prohibition had turned our cities into criminal shambles, and when, on the periphery of sanity, there were such curious excesses as marathon dancing and flagpole sitting, the patriotic societies fought constantly against "entangling alliances." We lost much in these ten years when we might have embraced the opportunity for world concert.

But the Sixth Column, supported now by the American Legion, the Veterans of Foreign Wars, and the Daughters of the American Revolution—to mention its most effective props—kept us in our frontier dream until the collapse of our economy brought us painfully to our senses.

Such an agonizing return to sanity has been a recurring phenomenon in American history. In these lucid intervals we are likely to revise our definition of patriotism.

II.   Sixth Columns in Europe

IN RUSSIA, years of struggle followed the disastrous treaty of Brest-Litovsk in March, 1918, in which the Russians ceded two thirds of their country. It is instructive, today, when we know so much more about what went on in that last year of the first World War than we did in turbulent 1919 and 1920, to realize that at the very time when Americans were most scared, Lenin had abandoned world revolution in order to save the revolution in Russia.[1] His stated policy was that this was mere postponement, not renunciation, of the Marxian plan for universal communism; a postponement which he believed necessary to bring order out of the chaos resulting from the internal revolution, the emergence of the new government and the new economy.

Through 1918, after the treaty between the Soviet government and that of Germany, the Bolsheviks occupied in Russia itself[2] only a fraction of what later came under their firm control. A part of the Russian armies had refused to accept the capitulation to the Germans and had remained loyal to the Allied cause.[3] The Allied War Council decided that Allied detachments should support these forces in trying to rebuild an eastern front and also to prevent supplies destined for the former Russian armed forces —then at Archangel and Vladivostok—from falling into German hands. Even with this help, however—at best half-hearted, es-

[1] Wheeler-Bennett, *op. cit.*, p. 147.
[2] C. Grove Haines and Ross J. S. Hoffman, *The Origins and Background of the Second World War*, New York: Oxford University Press, 1947, p. 65.
[3] *Ibid.*, p. 76.

pecially in the rugged northern winter—the so-called "White" armies failed in their effort and with the final defeat of Germany the Soviet government recovered all it had lost at Brest-Litovsk. But the intervention left a residue of bitterness on both sides that events of the succeeding years did not sweeten.

Through the decade of the 1920's Russian strength grew. The process of consolidating gains and compensating losses was a ruthless one; its incidents shocked the peoples of the western world. The liquidation of the bourgeoisie was brought about by brutalities that seemed unprecedented—at least since the Mongol operations of the thirteenth century. Two factors, however, made the creation of the enormous nation possible: one was the apathy of the Russian peoples, accustomed as they were to centuries of oppression under the Czars; the other was the sheer genius of Lenin[4] and, up to a certain point, the organizing abilities of Trotsky who produced the formidable Red Army.

It was natural that this growth of the new Russian power should spread alarm through the capitalist nations of Europe. Statesmen in the democracies were apprehensive of the tightening of the Soviet dictatorship, men with heavy vested interests were fearful lest the infection of nationalization become epidemic in their own economies, politicians dreaded the increase of Communist seats in their parliaments, and theologians were shocked by the Soviet anti-religious movement. The momentary easing of tension brought by Lenin's New Economic Policy was eventually counteracted by Stalin's liquidation of millions of kulaks under the farm collectivization program and, finally, by the purges of the 1930's within the Party which resulted in the execution of many of the revolution's foremost men.

Already, by the time Hitler came into power in Germany, fear of the Communist menace—in England and France at least—overshadowed any threat which might come with the growing power, in Central Europe, of the old enemy. Even the Nazi blood bath of 1934 when, with a brutality that Josef Stalin might well

[4] Leon Trotsky, *Lenin*, Garden City, New York: Garden City Books, 1959, *passim*.

have envied, Hitler and Goering murdered their former friends and supporters,[5] was mitigated, at least in certain British minds, by the Nazis' hatred of Russia and their liquidation of German Communists.

Looking back at the succession of Hitler's perfidies, broken promises, and sadistic cynicism, it seems incredible that any so-called statesman in a free democracy could have believed in his good faith. There was, however, a group in England, led by some of the foremost men in the British political arena, which became in the late 1930's a British Sixth Column that seemed to other Englishmen to be betraying not only their own country but civilization itself.

2

Whether the Cliveden set—named after the home of Lord and Lady Astor where it often met—sincerely believed that the Communists were a greater danger to the nation's security than the Nazis or were scared, rather, about the potential dissolution of their private fortunes mattered little in the result. In any case they were possessed by fear of the new, unpredictable Russian bear and, because Hitler felt as they did about Russia, were inclined to be pro-Nazi. The Germans, they said, were "more like us" and were bound to listen to reason, providing their Führer was properly approached. The opposition—persons who had read *Mein Kampf*—knew better. But those who were in power in England had not read this detailed prophecy of treachery by the past master of that art.[6]

Two successive prime ministers, Baldwin and Chamberlain, were more or less under the influence of the Sixth Column. Neville Chamberlain was completely dominated by it. So, too, were his cabinet ministers, many members of Parliament, and several ambassadors. The diplomats were shuffled toward the

[5] William L. Shirer, *The Rise and Fall of the Third Reich*, New York: Simon and Schuster, 1960, chap. 7.

[6] Alfred Leslie Rowse, *Appeasement: A Study in Political Decline*, New York: W. W. Norton Co., 1961, p. 31.

end of the decade so as to eliminate those who disagreed with their premier. According to Rowse, the Sixth Column was supported, editorially, by the *Times* of London.

Specifically, according to Alfred Leslie Rowse, whose *Appeasement: A Study in Political Decline* is a grim reminder of that dark era, the men at the hard core of the Chamberlain group were John Simon, Samuel Hoare, Thomas Jones, Lord Lothian, Arthur Salter, Lord Halifax, and the *Times* editors Robert Barrington-Ward and Geoffrey Dawson.[7] Most of these believed—or said they believed—even after the invasion of the Rhineland, the *Anschluss* in Austria, and the rape of Czechoslovakia—that they were "men of peace" and that the appeasement of Hitler would insure "peace in our time." "I sometimes wonder," writes Rowse, "whether more harm is done in the world by criminals or by good, moral men who lend themselves to their purposes."[8]

This Sixth Column was much encouraged by the German ambassador to London, Joachim von Ribbentrop. The Chamberlain group found him attractive and reasonable. Thomas Jones in his *Diary with Letters* wrote, recalling a meeting with the ambassador a month after Hitler's Rhineland venture:

> He talks English very well and I'm sure does not want war in the West. He talks of Hitler as being of quite superior attainments and fundamentally an artist, widely read, passionately devoted to music and pictures. They share dread of Russia. Communism is the enemy which Germany cannot resist alone and successfully without the help of Great Britain. France is succumbing to the bribery of Moscow; so is Spain. The Paris press and the French Deputies, a hundred of them, are in the pay of the Bolsheviks, so he assured me. . . .[9]

A somewhat different inference was drawn by Winston Churchill, in 1937, when he had a two-hour conversation with Ribbentrop at the ambassador's request.

[7] *Ibid.*, Appendix.
[8] *Ibid.*, p. 9.
[9] Thomas Jones, *A Diary with Letters*, London: Oxford University Press, 1954, p. 186.

What was required [Churchill wrote that Ribbentrop said] was that Britain should give Germany a free hand in the East of Europe. She must have her *Lebensraum* or living-space, for her increasing population. Therefore, Poland and the Danzig Corridor must be absorbed. White Russia and the Ukraine were indispensable to the future life of the German Reich. . . . Nothing less would suffice. All that was asked of the British Commonwealth and Empire was not to interfere. . . .

After hearing all this, I said at once that I was sure the British Government would not agree to give Germany a free hand in Eastern Europe. It was true we were on bad terms with Soviet Russia and that we hated Communism as much as Hitler did, but he might be sure that, even if France were safeguarded, Great Britain would never disinterest herself in the fortunes of the Continent to an extent which would enable Germany to gain the domination of Central and Eastern Europe. . . . Ribbentrop turned abruptly away. He then said, "In that case war is inevitable. There is no way out. The Fuehrer is resolved. Nothing will stop him and nothing will stop us."[1]

But Winston Churchill, at that time, was a voice crying in the wilderness. He was still an M.P., but the English people had rejected him as Prime Minister. It was true he led the opposition in the Commons but Government paid no attention to him. He reported his conversation with Ribbentrop to the Foreign Office[2] which filed his report away. Ribbentrop remained the confidant and friend of the Sixth Column until Hitler appointed him German Foreign Secretary. Then, as he was about to leave London, Chamberlain gave him a farewell luncheon at 10 Downing Street. The luncheon occurred on the very day that Hitler invaded Austria and Ribbentrop was handed a telegram with the news while the genial party went on. Churchill was present.

This was the last time [he wrote] I saw Herr von Ribbentrop before he was hanged.[3]

[1] Winston S. Churchill, *The Gathering Storm*, Boston: Houghton Mifflin Co., 1948, p. 223.
[2] *Ibid.*, p. 224.
[3] *Ibid.*, p. 272.

Following Hitler's subjugation of Vienna, Churchill said in the Commons:

> The gravity of the event of March 12 [1938] cannot be exaggerated. Europe is confronted with a programme of aggression, nicely calculated and timed, unfolding stage by stage, and there is only one choice open, not only to us but to other countries, either to submit like Austria, or else take effective measures while time remains to ward off the danger. . . . How many times will bluff succeed until behind bluff ever-gathering forces have accumulated reality? . . . *Where are we going to be two years hence, for instance, when the German Army will certainly be larger than the French Army,* and when all the small nations have fled from Geneva to pay homage to the ever-waxing power of the Nazi system, and to make the best terms they can for themselves?[4] [Italics in original.]

He continued, in the same speech, to warn of the danger to Czechoslovakia, next, probably, on Hitler's list. But Chamberlain and his group were determined to play Hitler's game. It was, indeed, not long after this that they began to listen sympathetically to the first Nazi arguments that led, with the assistance of the British Sixth Column, to Hitler's attack on the Czechoslovak republic.

3

Documents later captured from the Germans show that Hitler's plan for the annexation of the Czech Sudetenland as a prelude to his occupation of the entire country was already complete in the summer of 1938. They also show the existence in Germany of a plot against the Führer by a group of his generals. The impulse for this betrayal of their leader was based on the belief of these military men that his plan could not possibly succeed and that if the German army obeyed his command to pursue this attack it would be destroyed.[5]

[4] *Ibid.*, p. 272.
[5] Shirer, *op. cit.*, pp. 372*ff*.

There was reason for these fears. It seemed certain to them that France, England, and Russia would unite in the defense of Czechoslovakia. They could not believe that France would not honor its promise to defend the Czechs or that the Franco-Soviet treaty would be broken. That Britain would not, at this perilous juncture, accept the offers the Soviet government had already made to the British government to form with it and France an alliance for collective security seemed, to these realists, inconceivable. With such a coalition against them the advance of the Nazis would be obviously impossible.

The Sixth Column, however, had already taken care of that. Churchill tells us that, immediately after the invasion of Austria:

> It was the Russians who now sounded the alarm, and on March 18 proposed a conference on the situation. They wished to discuss, if only in outline, ways and means of implementing the Franco-Soviet Pact within the frame of League action in the event of a major threat to peace by Germany. This met with little warmth in Paris and London. The French Government was distracted by other preoccupations. There were serious strikes in the aircraft factories. Franco's armies were driving deep into the territory of Communist Spain. Chamberlain was both sceptical and depressed. He profoundly disagreed with my interpretation of the dangers ahead and the means of combating them. I had been urging the prospects of a Franco-British-Russian alliance as the only hope of checking the Nazi onrush.[6]

A week later, Chamberlain said in Commons:

> His Majesty's Government are of the opinion that the indirect but none the less inevitable consequence of such action as is proposed by the Soviet Government would be to aggravate the tendency towards the establishment of exclusive groups of nations which must in the view of His Majesty's Government be inimical to the prospects of European peace.[7]

[6] Churchill, *op. cit.*, p. 274.
[7] *Ibid.*, p. 275.

41

This echo from Cliveden was soon heard in Berlin and it gave assurance to Hitler. On May 28, he

ordered (1) that preparations should be made for military action against this [Czechoslovak] state by October 2; and (2) the immense and accelerated expansion of our defensive front in the West.[8]

The following month, however, the Führer, aware of the anxiety of his generals though not of their plot against him, wrote to his Chief of Staff, General Wilhelm Keitel:

I will decide to take action against Czechoslovakia only if I am firmly convinced, as in the case of the demilitarized zone [the Rhineland] and the entry into Austria, that France will not march, and that therefore England will not intervene.[9]

The anxiety of the conspirators was not, however, quieted. Churchill's opposition to the Sixth Column had impressed them and Churchill, generally, had impressed them more than he had the British people. The plotters agreed that the time to overthrow Hitler was "the moment he gave the word to attack."[1] But as time went on, word got to Germany of the British government's persistent effort to induce the Czech government to concede the partition of their republic, giving the Sudeten area, said to be mainly populated by Germans, to Germany. If the British were successful here and, if they thus met Hitler's demand for this cession, the chance of bloodshed would be averted and the plot of the mutinous generals would fail. General Halder, key man in the conspiracy, was therefore anxious that Churchill should prevail and that he, Halder, would be assured of a firm stand by Britain and France. By various indirect means, Halder had tried to get such an assurance from London. But

[8] Speech to the Reichstag, Jan. 30, 1939. Shirer, *op. cit.*, p. 365.
[9] Nuremberg Documents, part 2, p. 10. Churchill, *op cit.*, p. 290.
[1] Shirer, *op. cit.*, pp. 378, 379.

General Halder had a feeling that the conspirators were not getting their message through effectively enough to the British, and on September 2 [1938] he sent his own emissary, a retired Army officer, Lieutenant Colonel Hans Boehm-Tettelbach, to London to make contact with the British War Office and Military Intelligence. Though, according to his own story, the colonel saw several important personages in London, he does not seem to have made much of an impression on them.[2]

The conspirators, though depressed by this result, did not despair. They had confederates in the German Foreign Office. Baron von Weizsaecker, described by William Shirer as "the brains of the Foreign Office," was, it is clear from captured documents, opposed at that time to "aggression against Czechoslovakia on the same grounds as those of the generals that it would lead to a lost war." There was also, in the German embassy at London, a sympathetic person named Theodor Kordt, who was counselor of the embassy and chargé d'affaires. As a final attempt,

it was agreed that Theodor Kordt should sound a last warning to Downing Street. As counselor of the embassy his visits to the British authorities would not be suspect.

The information he brought on the evening of September 5 to Sir Horace Wilson, Chamberlain's confidential adviser, seemed so important and urgent that this official spirited him by a back way to Downing Street and the chambers of the British Foreign Secretary. There he bluntly informed Lord Halifax that Hitler was planning to order a general mobilization on September 16, that the attack on Czechoslovakia had been fixed for October 1 at the latest, that the German Army was preparing to strike against Hitler the moment the final order for attack was given and that it would succeed if Britain and France held firm. Halifax also warned that Hitler's speech closing the Nuremberg Party Rally on September 12 would be explosive and might precipitate a showdown over Czecho-

[2] *Ibid.*, p. 381.

slovakia and that would be the moment for Britain to stand up against the dictator.[3]

The Chamberlain government was therefore given the opportunity to change the whole course of history. But the Sixth Column had other plans. The Prime Minister was convinced, after his Cliveden meetings, that war could be avoided by meeting the Führer's first demand—the cession of the Sudetenland—on condition that Hitler would promise no further aggression.

The German generals knew, of course, that in the area Hitler demanded lay Czechoslovakia's natural defense; that Hitler made the demand, not because of the German population there but because, once he occupied this natural fortress, the republic would be so weakened that occupation of the whole would then be easy. He therefore sent his celebrated invitation to Chamberlain and Chamberlain returned his notorious acceptance.

> In view of the increasingly critical situation I propose to come over at once to see you with a view to trying to find a peaceful solution.[4]

The following tragedy of Munich is too well known a page of history to need repetition here. What was not well known before the publication of Mr. Shirer's book, based on an exhaustive study of captured documents and of the testimony given at the Nuremberg trials, was the detailed story of the army plot to overthrow Hitler and its defeat by Chamberlain.

At the final interview between the Prime Minister and the Führer, both the French and the Italians were represented. Hitler had invited them to come. "No invitation was sent to Prague or Moscow. Russia, the coguarantor of Czechoslovakia's integrity in case of a German attack, was not to be allowed to interfere. The Czechs were not even asked to be present at their own sen-

---

[3] *Ibid.*, p. 382.
[4] *Ibid.*, p. 384. Documents on German Foreign Policy, II, p. 754.

tence."[5] Although Hitler had looked forward to an immediate military attack and victory over the Czechs, the offers of the French and British to sell Czechoslovakia down the river for a promise of peace were irresistible and he accepted them.

At the Nuremberg trials in 1946, General Halder was interrogated about the collapse of the army conspiracy against the leader.

It had been planned [said Halder] to occupy by military force the Reichs Chancellery and those government offices, particularly ministries, which were administered by party members and close supporters of Hitler, with the express intention of avoiding bloodshed and then trying the group before the whole German nation. . . . On the day [September 28] Witzleben came to see me in my office during the noon hour. We discussed the matter. He requested that I give him the order of execution. . . . During this discussion, the news came that the British Prime Minister and the French premier had agreed to come to Hitler for further talks. . . . I therefore took back the order of execution because, owing to this fact, the entire basis for the action had been taken away.

We were firmly convinced that we would be successful. But now came Mr. Chamberlain and with one stroke the danger of war was averted. . . . The critical hour for force was avoided. . . .

The examiner, Captain Sam Harris, a New York attorney, then asked the general:

Do I understand you to say that if Chamberlain had not come to Munich, your plan would have been executed, and Hitler would have been deposed?

I can only say the plan would have been executed [General Halder replied]. I do not know if it would have been successful.[6]

[5] Shirer, op. cit., pp. 409–10.
[6] From Halder's interrogation Feb. 25, 1946, Nazi Conspiracy and

The military attack was, of course, merely postponed until Hitler had consolidated his jumping-off place in the Sudetenland beyond the mountain barrier that was Czechoslovakia's only natural defense. It took place in March, 1939, and the Führer himself rode proudly into Prague.

Yet even then, even after Munich, even after the unopposed invasion of the Czech republic, Chamberlain and the Sixth Column still believed they had bought peace for England and France, and Churchill was still fighting for his last hope of bringing Russia into a collective defense.

4

In March, 1939, immediately after Hitler's invasion, the Russian Government, "profoundly affected by all that was taking place, proposed a Six-Power Conference." But Chamberlain turned away from the idea. In a private letter he wrote:

> I must confess to the most profound distrust of Russia. I have no belief whatever in her ability to maintain an effective offensive, even if she wanted to. And I distrust her motives, which seem to me to have little connection with our ideas of liberty, and to be concerned only with getting everyone else by the ears.[7]

But Churchill persisted. Observing the coolness with which this like all other offers from the Soviets had been received, he said:

> I have been quite unable to understand what is the objection to making the agreement with Russia . . . and making it in the broad and simple form proposed by the Russian Soviet Government.

Undoubtedly, the proposals put forward by the Russian

Aggression. (Part of the Nuremberg Documents.) Supplement B, pp. 1553–58. Shirer, *op. cit.*, p. 412.

[7] Churchill, *op. cit.*, p. 349.

Government contemplate a triple alliance against aggression between England, France, and Russia. . . . The alliance is solely for the purpose of resisting further acts of aggression and of protecting the victims of aggression. I cannot see what is wrong with that. What is wrong with this simple proposal? It is said, "Can you trust the Russian Soviet Government?" I suppose in Moscow they say, "Can we trust Chamberlain?" I hope we may say that the answer to both questions is in the affirmative. I earnestly hope so.[8]

Nevertheless, the final Russian offer was not accepted although, for a moment, when it was too late, Chamberlain seemed to weaken and said he was not irrevocably opposed to some sort of alliance. This time, however, the Soviets were no longer willing to wait for the Prime Minister to make up his mind. It was a propitious moment for the Nazis to suggest that all might be forgiven and forgotten if, in the interests of realism, they joined forces with the Germans—or, at least agreed to remain neutral. The German Foreign Office pursued this objective with urgency as it appeared to them that pressure was being brought upon Chamberlain to alter his views. Thus, in midsummer, 1939, a wire was sent to the German ambassador in Moscow urging him, "in view of the political situation and in the interests of speed," to suggest to the Russian Foreign Office a continuation of "the conversations on harmonizing German-Soviet intentions."[9]

As a result of this cynical approach, there was signed, on August 24, the ten-year non-aggression pact which so shocked the western world. That the British Sixth Column, joined by a belated one in France, thus forced the Soviets into the arms of the Nazis, can scarcely, in view of the German secret documents, be doubted. A week after the signing, Hitler invaded Poland and annexed Danzig.

[8] Churchill, *op. cit.*, pp. 373–74.
[9] Documents on German Foreign Policy, VI, pp. 1048–49. Shirer, *op. cit.*, p. 505.

III. Depression and New Deal

WHILE THE INTENT OF the Sixth Column in the United States has been to raise American prestige in American eyes, the effect of its acts has been to lower it in the foreign view. We have begun, in the 1960's, to worry about this. Both diplomats and tourists have met a hostility abroad that is in sharp contrast to American self-confidence and national pride. But as we explore the conduct of the column over the past four or five decades, it is not hard to see the reasons for the loss of foreign esteem. For, in the difficult transition that world events have forced upon us, from isolation to a part in the international scene, we have, indeed, sold ourselves down the river.

Twice we have let the opportunity for world leadership slip away from us because the Sixth Column has scared us into inaction. We emerged from the first World War stronger than we had ever been and stronger than our allies. We had roused in Europe—especially France—an admiration that was almost mystic. When, in the early months of 1919, our President drove through the streets of Paris women knelt before the new Messiah. But we returned from the fight against Germany to fight among ourselves. Of the League of Nations, which was regarded in many foreign quarters as the hope of mankind, we made a political football that held our controversial attention while the opportunity lapsed.

The Red Scare, implemented by the Palmer raids, was a spectacular symptom of our return to isolationism in the face of a new world complex. At a time when a considerable percentage of our thought should, by all the portents, have been international, we were frightened into what was known as "hundred per cent Americanism." The post-war hysteria erased most of the good that had come to us from the association with alien peoples—the unity in a common cause with other free and democratic nations.

The epidemic of fear was watched from abroad with incredulous surprise. As the panic began to abate early in 1921, one of its consequences came in a travesty of American justice that shocked the world. Two Italians with radical backgrounds were tried, convicted of murder, and sentenced to death. It is true that Nicola Sacco and Bartolomeo Vanzetti were anarchists and had advocated obstructing the war effort. If they had been tried for those offenses, convicted and sentenced to the appropriate punishment, there would have been no repercussions. But to be tried for murder and convicted because they were anarchists—which is what has come to be generally believed—was not orthodox judicial procedure in a democracy.

The protests were so wide, so loud, and so long that the execution was delayed for six years. They came from England, from the continent of Europe, from Latin America. Liberals in the United States accused the judge, the jury, and the prosecution of prejudice. Legal experts examined the evidence by which the prosecution attempted to prove that these unhappy men had held up and killed the paymaster of a Massachusetts shoe factory and his guard, and pronounced it wholly inadequate.

On appeal, it was "found" that there had been no irregularities in the trial. The defendants were unable to take the case to a higher court. Eventually such pressure was brought on Governor Alvan Fuller of Massachusetts to pardon the men that he appointed a commission of highly respected and respectable citizens to advise him. These persons: Presidents A. Lawrence Lowell of Harvard and Samuel Wesley Stratton of the Massachusetts Institute of Technology and Judge Robert Grant of Boston, a former probate judge, could find no warrant for pardoning Sacco and Vanzetti and they went to their death in

August, 1927. Letters they had written before they were executed revealed them as sensitive men, widely read, and with strong desires toward education who would be unlikely to kill from a robbery motive.

The case has been compared with the Dreyfus affair in France and several books have been written about it including one by Felix Frankfurter.[1] "The drama of such an affair as this" wrote H. N. Brailsford in the *New Leader*, "will make 'radicals' where volumes of economic argument would fail."[2]

2

As the decade wore on and American society reverted more and more to the frontier phase, many domestic preoccupations confirmed their isolationism. There was national prohibition with its corollaries of crime and hypocrisy; there were the oil scandals involving officials in the highest government echelons; there was the death of President Harding, victim of the forces his election had conjured up and most potent, perhaps, of all, there was the financial boom making paper millionaires overnight. In the midst of these dreams which turned, at last, to nightmares, we sent emissaries abroad to crystallize the myth of "the war to end war" by means of "pacts" which should "outlaw" armed international conflict—the term "outlaw" being borrowed from the cattle range of the frontier.

The upshot of this effort to regain a lost international leadership was the Pact of Paris (better known as Kellogg-Briand) of which the historians Morison and Commager had this to say about the naiveté (or hypocrisy) of the sixty-two nations which adhered to it:

The most thoroughgoing commitment to peace which great

[1] Felix Frankfurter, *The Case of Sacco and Vanzetti*, Boston: Little, Brown & Co., 1927.

[2] Aug. 12, 1927. Quoted by George L. Joughin and Edmund M. Morgan, *The Legacy of Sacco and Vanzetti*, New York: Harcourt, Brace & Co., 1948, p. 289. This is probably the best work on the aftermath of the affair that has yet appeared.

powers had ever made, the Pact of Paris was completely lacking in sanctions, and not even its sponsors appeared to believe in its effectiveness.[3]

The same authors commented that on the day the United States Senate ratified the treaty by a vote of 81 to 1, that body "took up consideration of a bill authorizing the construction of fifteen cruisers."

Mr. Coolidge was then in the White House, presiding over an era of prosperity only paralleled in the days of frontier wealth, the difference being that the Comstock Lode yielded gold whereas the stock exchanges of the 1920's yielded only promissory notes. Mr. Coolidge encouraged the notion that all this good fortune was the result of that fine old Yankee virtue, thrift. He knew better, of course, and got out just in time.

While all this was going on, two European forces were building strength. The Soviet Union consolidated its gains, compensated its losses by prodigious labor and eliminated its weaknesses along with the Russian bourgeoisie. It established the dictatorship of the proletariat by the simple expedient of depriving the workers of all power and it betrayed its own revolution by establishing the foundation of an empire. At the other end of Europe—the Mediterranean tip—a political party that called itself "fascist" achieved a similar authoritarian government and covered up its similarity to communism by declaring its eternal enmity to it.

At the beginning of 1929, Americans in their grandiose mood were disposed to applaud Mussolini for promoting order in a country which Americans believed had always been chaotic, but particularly for his change of heart from socialism to angry anti-communism. They were so disposed, that is, if they thought about it at all, which in that frenzied summer of 1929 they were unlikely to do. Then, in October, they woke abruptly to realities.

In the years that followed, the Sixth Column virtually dis-

[3] Samuel E. Morison and Henry S. Commager, *The Growth of the American Republic*, New York: Oxford University Press, 1937, vol. II, p. 500.

appeared from the United States. American thinking altered. Americans, instead of regarding themselves as one hundred per cent American, tended, or wanted, to think of themselves as one hundred per cent human. Emphasis on nationality or party or religion or ethnic group gave way to preoccupation with common suffering. We were all, to be sure, in the same boat, adrift on a sea of misery.

It was a propitious time for communists to agitate. The Party is normally fed by hunger, poverty, and discontent. It made some gains, of course, in America during the Great Depression, but surprisingly few. Some intellectuals and some psychopaths, such as Whittaker Chambers and other champions of a later Sixth Column, joined the Party and, according to their own accounts, attempted espionage and the spread of subversion, but with very little success. The masses were not looking to communism as their savior; the industrial workers had already became distrustful of it since the Soviet government had emasculated the unions. The unemployed stood patiently on breadlines or settled down in communities they ironically called Hoovervilles after their chicken-in-every-pot President; ate out of garbage cans and were carried away by ambulances. There was talk of revolution, to be sure, especially among scared right-wingers; there was some talk of it among the hungry, too, but it was not communist revolution; in 1932, it turned into a political unheaval and there were ballots rather than bombs.[4]

There was no room for traitors in these years in America; there seemed to be nothing left to betray. The people had lost faith in themselves and in their institutions which appeared already to have betrayed them. They lived from day to day in the deep valleys without hope. But in the spring of 1933 when the White House sheltered a new tenant, a glimmer of it came with the promise of a new deal.

After his inaugural, Franklin Roosevelt had the nation behind

[4] Dixon Wecter, *The Age of the Great Depression*, New York: The Macmillan Co., 1948. "To the ballot box rather than the soap box most citizens looked when they wanted a change," p. 38.

him. Even those who had opposed him at the polls gave him
their trust. With the first steps toward recovery there seemed to
be an awakening of life through the people.

But when recovery came, the Sixth Column came with it.

3

President Roosevelt had nearly universal support until he
"betrayed his class." There were still Americans in 1932, after a
century and a half of advance toward the concept of equality
presented in the Declaration of Independence, who took this
matter of class seriously. Precisely on what they based their
belief in their theory of social hierarchy is not clear. Obviously
it was not nobility, for many who thought of themselves as
American aristocrats did so because they could trace their descent from a servant who arrived on the *Mayflower* or other early
immigrant vessel. It was not, they stoutly maintained, a matter
of money though many of the "best people" lived in considerable
comfort on fine old estates. Nor was it because of a pedigree of
unblemished honor. Surely many sons and daughters of the
American Revolution would not care to have the service records
of their patriot ancestors too carefully scanned, though desertion
and other military offenses were regarded more tolerantly then
than now.

Franklin Roosevelt came from an old and, on the whole, honorable New York family. The early Roosevelts were, for the most
part, artisans who worked with their hands, but so did most
Americans in colonial times. More important, the Roosevelts
from whom Franklin immediately descended owned a large
estate on the Hudson River, once dominated by Dutch patroons.
Inherited wealth filled out the picture for those who were concerned with "class." In view of all these assets, even the stigma
of being a Democrat could be forgiven.

The first drastic steps to alleviate the more acute pains of the
Depression reflected no treason to the President's class. On the
contrary, the National Industrial Recovery Act which he promoted encouraged the businessmen who favored monopoly. Many

of its provisions such as those instituting codes for entire indus-
tries reduced competition, permitted price-fixing, and relieved
corporations from attack under the anti-trust acts. These pleased
the tycoons. Among them there was, at first, much enthusiasm.
There were parades, speeches, band playing, and a special flag
for those who co-operated. But the favorable response was
dampened for the industrialists by the relief provisions which
the President included in the plan, to complement the stimulus
to business. The time came when employers could not stomach
those sections which shortened hours, put a floor under wages,
abolished child labor, and, worst of all, provided for collective
bargaining.

NRA, as the title became shortened to, came under attack from
all sides. Small businessmen thought it squeezed out small
business. Even the workers, while favoring the restraints on
management, resented the monopolistic aspects which caused a
rise in the cost of living. The protests grew loud and strong.

But there was no Sixth Column yet. Criticism of the government and of the president was in the American tradition:
democracy would be impossible without it. And, indeed, there
was much to criticize in this institution which seemed to exceed
the constitutional powers of the executive. Even NRA's defenders
were forced into a defensive, even an apologetic, posture, explaining that it was, at least, a demonstration of action in a crisis
of dead center. So there was general relief when the Supreme
Court declared the act unconstitutional and the whole ungainly
structure collapsed.

An effort to revive the Sixth Column was made by Elizabeth
Dilling in the private publication of a volume called *The Red
Network* (1934) which included a "Who's Who in Radicalism."
Listing such names as Eleanor Roosevelt, Newton D. Baker,
Albert Einstein, Clifton Fadiman, and Harry Emerson Fosdick,
the book merely aroused ridicule and many respectable citizens
were proud to have their names included. But already an arsenal
of ammunition had accumulated for future columns. And soon
after, scared men began putting one together.

Any attempt to bolster labor by giving it new rights and new freedoms; any restraint upon the excesses of capitalism; any payment to persons who did not earn it, however great their suffering and however impossible their finding a job, smelled in some nostrils like communism. It was to such precincts of prejudice that the Sixth Column returned. There it remained— even to the threshold of the new war—and was often in close proximity to its neighbor the Fifth. Its effect, however, differed from that of the 1920's in that it never reached anything approaching a majority of Americans until the Congress gave it official standing after the war was over.

Its first activity was the diffusion of backstairs gossip in a wide whispering operation. The President, it appeared, was under constant surveillance by a group of alienists. These doctors were often disguised as servants in the White House staff. On several occasions when the head of state went berserk, it had been necessary to apply a strait jacket. In spite of every effort to keep these unhappy episodes a secret, the awful truth had leaked out. Our family physician, ran the talk over coffee and liqueurs on Park Avenue, got this direct at a meeting of the A.M.A. at which one of these insanity experts had been present. Or, as a variant, our butler has a cousin on the President's personal staff. Or, one of these shocking incidents occurred during an official visit of a close friend of our brother's who, you know, is high up in the State Department.

Everyone knows, of course, that the President has a pathological Oedipus or "silver cord" complex. Poor Eleanor (though Eleanor, in other contexts, came in for a variety of poison whispers) has suffered for years under this burden. But there can be no question that both domestic and foreign policies are dictated by Sara Delano (Mrs. James) Roosevelt, a clever woman but an essentially vicious one. We have this direct from a sister of a classmate of Eleanor's brother, Hall.

And so on. It is an old story. Wilson had a social disease, Theodore Roosevelt and Andrew Johnson were drunkards, Grant was rarely if ever sober, Jefferson was the father of a mulatto

55

bastard. In Franklin Roosevelt's case, the whispering Sixth Column operated mainly within his own "class" the members of which saw the idolatry accorded him by a large part of the electorate as a symptom of national decay.

As always, some of the bitterest opponents of President Roosevelt refused to listen to these whispers. They had, they believed, in NRA, in the Supreme Court "packing," in the "coddling" of labor, in the encouragement of boondoggling, in the recognition of the U.S.S.R., and in his antagonism toward big business, reasons for their bitterness that needed no bolstering by obscene rumor. These were honorable and decent citizens who must never be confused with the members of the Sixth Column.

4

When the second World War began in Europe, there was a natural effort, in the United States, to revive the myth of isolation. The nation had, indeed, been protected by its oceans plus the British navy for a good many years. In 1917, the isolationists said, we had been lured out of that protection by the cynical politicians of Europe who wanted us to "pull their chestnuts out of the fire." And what had come of it? Nothing but a setback to our politics and our economy, not to mention the death and crippling of our "boys."

More thoughtful students of recent American history believed that the myth of physical isolation had been exploded when Billy Mitchell had sunk obsolete capital ships of the navy by dropping bombs on them from airplanes. And yet, in the confused years of 1940 and 1941, America's number-one aviator, Charles Lindbergh, who, himself, had demonstrated the feasibility of flying solo across the Atlantic, became an isolationist leader!

The war brought back an outbreak of that debatable patriotism best expressed by the slogan "America First." Already the term "American" had been given a highly parochial connotation when, in 1938, the House of Representatives had authorized a committee to inquire into "un-American" activities. The latitude

56

accorded this committee may be guessed from the large variety of doings to which the adjective "American" may be applied. What is an "American" activity? What "un-American?" This is a matter of more personal and private definition than, for example, "unrighteous," "ungodly," or "unorthodox." If you dislike or disapprove of someone, you may call him and all his works "un-American" and who can prove or disprove so vague an accusation? And when such allegations are given official sanction it concentrates a good deal of discriminatory power. The birth of this committee is the most convincing evidence we have of the revival of the Sixth Column in the United States.

The desire to keep out of the war that followed the Russo-German pact in 1939 was a normal one for Americans. The average citizen hated war on principle. Many looked upon the last war as spiritually disastrous for the nation. We had suffered little, materially, but this very fact had obligated us to leadership or at least co-operation in the pursuit of a just and enduring peace—a debt we had not paid. Were we to go deeper in moral debt by joining in this new Armageddon? Yet was that not, perhaps, the only way we could make restitution for the losses we had caused? Were we not, by our refusal to join the League, partly responsible for the present conflict?

So, through the summer of 1940, the controversy harassed the American conscience. But as the Netherlands, Belgium, and France fell under ruthless Nazi attack, it was also normal for Americans to feel a deep sympathy for the victims and an admiration for British courage in the face of the grievous odds. As this view became shared by a majority of Americans, the group that called itself the America First Committee stepped in.

If this group had confined its activity to legitimate and logical anti-intervention propaganda it might have escaped the stigma of joining the Sixth Column. Many sincere and honest Americans sympathized with its aims. But as it felt the tide turning against it, it betrayed the traditional American ideology. Its publicists abused our potential allies, the peoples who thought, as we did, in the directions of freedom and who were being defeated

57

by totalitarian forces whose headlong advance had left a trail of blood and suffering such as the modern world had never known. Further, vocalists of the America First Committee, in speech after speech, condoned Nazi brutality and took so definite a pro-German stand that it became infiltrated by persons whom the FBI soon recognized as potential spies and saboteurs. Finally, they bitterly criticized the President's preparedness measures and accused him of "war-mongering." Meanwhile, on Capitol Hill, the Congress had again become busy investigating.

5

The special Un-American Activities Committee created by the House of Representatives on May 4, 1938, had in its ancestry another group dedicated to inquiry into subversion. This was a special group appointed in 1930 by a House resolution

> to investigate communist propaganda in the United States and particularly in our educational institutions; the activities and membership of the Communist Party of the United States and all affiliated organizations and groups thereof; the ramification of the Communist International in the United States; the Amtorg Trading Corporation; the Daily Worker, and all entities, groups, or individuals who are alleged to advise, teach, or advocate the overthrow by force or violence of the Government of the United States, or attempt to undermine our republican form of government by inciting riots, sabotage, or revolutionary disorders.[5]

This was so large an order that only Representative Hamilton Fish, Republican, of New York, who had the most sensitive nose for the scent of Communist subversion of anyone in the country, could handle it. Nevertheless his committee after several hearings produced only negative findings. There was no evidence to support the wild charges that had been made against the Party, its paper, and its commercial corporations; so the committee's

[5] 72 CR 9390, May 22, 1930. HR 220.

report had to compensate for this lack by drastic recommendations for legislation designed to abolish the Party. Almost nothing was done by the lawmakers in consequence. There was much else to think about in 1930 and by 1934 after Hitler's initial successes, Congress found the Nazi propaganda a momentarily distracting topic.

The Congress, however, could never quite forget communism. The subject was kept alive no doubt by the wealthier constituents of many western representatives who lived in a perpetual climate of fear and preferred to be frightened by the Russian rather than the German menace. Congressman Martin Dies whose state, Texas, boasted huge vested interests in petroleum and other resources, was especially restive. Foremost among those urging the House to create the special Un-American Activities Committee in 1938, Dies became its chairman.

In view of its later performance, the views of Dies at its inception are remarkable for their awareness of the dangers of such a committee.

I can conceive [he said] that a committee constituted of men whose object is to gain publicity, or whose object it is to arouse hatred against some race or creed, or to do things of that sort, might do more harm than good. . . . Always we must keep in mind that in any legislative attempt to prevent un-American activities, we might jeopardize fundamental rights far more important than the objective we seek. . . .[6]

At the committee's first hearing in midsummer, 1938, Dies said:

This committee will not permit any "character assassination" or any "smearing" of innocent people. We wish to caution witnesses that reckless charges must not be made against any individual or organization. . . .

The most common practice engaged in by some people is to brand their opponents with names when they are unable to refute their arguments with facts and logic. Therefore, we

[6] 83 CR 7569, 7570, May 26, 1938.

59

find a few people of conservative thought who are inclined to brand every liberal viewpoint as communistic. Likewise we find some so-called liberals who stigmatize every conservative idea [as] fascistic. The utmost care, therefore, must be observed to distinguish clearly between what is obviously un-American and what is no more or less than an honest difference of opinion with respect to some economic, political, or social question.[7]

Notwithstanding this cautious approach, the wording of the resolution offered the new committee not only an opportunity to disregard all the cautions but virtually a directive to ignore them. The resolution called for a seven-man committee to investigate:

(1) The extent, character, and objects of un-American propaganda activities in the United States, (2) the diffusion within the United States of subversive and un-American propaganda that is instigated from foreign countries or of a domestic origin and attacks the principle of the form of government as guaranteed by our Constitution, and (3) all other questions in relation thereto that would aid Congress in any necessary remedial legislation.[8]

It does not require unduly logical thinking to realize that any word coming from overseas is inherently un-American. A French cookbook, for example, that specified that steak should be served rare would be un-American in the extreme; an even more subversive example would be an item of British propaganda attacking the use of ice in whiskey or mixed drinks.

The debate in the House on this resolution as reported in the *Congressional Record* reads much like a passage from Lewis Carroll; the quiet reasonable voice of Alice being constantly interrupted by hysterical cries of "Off with their heads!" In the

[7] Hearings before the Special Committee on Un-American Activities, 75th Cong., 3d Sess., Aug. 12, 1938, vol. I, pp. 1, 2, 3.
[8] HR 282, 75th Cong., 3d Sess.

House Wonderland, however, such antiphonies are not unusual as the most casual reading of that fascinating document, the *Congressional Record*, reveals.

Anti-communism had a new flare-up following the Stalin-Hitler pact of 1939, and especially during the winter Russo-Finnish war; yet the strong anti-Russian wave that swept the nation as a result of these events was healthy. Most of those Americans who had been in sympathy with the Russian revolution severed all connection with the Party. Though some of these abruptly disillusioned persons later became members of the Sixth Column and engaged in extremes of character assassination, others proved extremely useful to the FBI and the Department of Justice. In general, as the war came nearer to American shores, a wholesome anger replaced the fear that had once weakened us.

It was, to be sure, no time for fear and after Pearl Harbor had dissolved the isolationist Sixth Column, the American people rose to peaks of courage and sacrifice unprecedented in American history. Yet when, at last, at war's end, the opportunity for world leadership was again in our hands, we let it slip away a second time.

IV. Legion

THOSE WHO HAILED THE BIRTH of the American Legion in 1919 hardly foresaw that this organization would one day advocate the stifling of freedoms guaranteed by the American Constitution. Yet any accurate review of the Legion's history reveals a series of episodes in which, in the name of patriotism, it has forcibly interrupted free speech and, by pressure implying the threat of violence, has subverted the freedom of the press. It has more than once forced the resignation or discharge of teachers who had the courage of their convictions and spoke their minds in the cause of peace and it has purged schools of their textbooks.

The American Legion has constantly demanded and obtained unwarranted benefits for veterans; it has discriminated against the widows and orphans of dead soldiers in order to insure payment of bonuses and other benefits to living veterans whose votes are necessary to the Legion's support and to its political ventures. It has maintained a well-paid lobby to influence federal legislation in its favor and it has supported the investigating committees of Congress in their character-assassination activities. These things it has done in the name of Americanism.[1]

The rank and file of the membership is not unanimously in sympathy with the Legion's chauvinism and predations. There has been much dissension. One entire post withdrew its support.[2]

[1] Roger Burlingame, *Peace Veterans*, New York: Minton, Balch & Co., 1932, *passim*. Knowlton Durham, *Billions for Veterans*, New York: Brewer, Warren & Putnam, 1932, *passim*.

[2] The Willard Straight Post, New York.

Many members have resigned to join other veterans' associations which they believed had the nation's greater good at heart. Other members who have kept their membership resent the arbitrary acts of their leaders and the "steam roller" tactics with which resolutions are adopted. Still others, while disapproving, cannot bring themselves to separate from an institution which has proved so financially profitable to its members.

There are psychological explanations for the success of the Legion and other societies which have their origins in military patriotism such as the Veterans of the Foreign Wars, the Daughters of the American Revolution, and the Grand Army of the Republic. The fact that the United States was victorious in all the wars that these represent is a source of pride even to those remotely connected with them. The aristocratic ladies who can trace their ancestry to a drummer boy in the Continental Army find a vicarious thrill in the star-spangled knowledge; furthermore such ancestry gives them a sense of power over their less fortunate fellow-citizens. But for those who actually did the shooting and were shot at themselves there is either a nostalgia for the fighting or a belief that they must still uphold the convictions for which they think they fought. For many, "that war" was the greatest thing in all their lives; the memory of it must be kept quick for their morale has no other prop.

It is an instructive fact, however, that the Legion owes most of its jingoist support to the non-combat veterans of the World Wars. At war's end, the discontented soldiers who had fought the battle of Washington or the Presidio were much relieved to find they had the same standing in the Legion as those who had taken an active part in the Aisne-Marne or Argonne or North African offensives. Most of these men who had sincerely wanted to go overseas were, after the victories, more warlike than those who had suffered the toil and sweat of real battle and were tired of it. From the beginning, the Legion's shrewd organizers were keenly aware that by far the largest percentage of ex-soldiers had never seen combat; they knew, therefore, that it would be the non-combatants who would insure the Legion's future and that these must never be permitted any sense of inferiority.

63

Though its membership has never included a majority of eligible former servicemen,[3] the Legion has consistently maintained that it represents the American veteran, and expresses, in its resolutions, his point of view on war and peace, on "Americanism" and subversion, on liberalism and conservatism, and on its political campaigns designed to pack the Congress with Legionnaires or with those who share the Legion's tenets.

Those outsiders who, in spite of every inducement, have refused to join the Legion, have become increasingly shocked by its behavior. Annually, they have watched some Convention city turned for four days into a barroom brawl in which the memory of a service they have taken seriously is exploited as sanction for unrestrained clowning and for every license including drunkenness and obscenity.[4] They have seen whole communities so dominated by Legion intimidation that no one dared speak out against the persecution of innocent men and women charged with subversion and they have suffered under the new tax burdens imposed by legislation the Legion has sponsored or, on occasions, jammed through Congress. It is not surprising, then, that they have persuaded many Legionnaires to defect to another veteran organization which believed that the entire citizenry of the United States was not composed of veterans and should not be regimented by a veteran dictatorship.

The fact of dictatorship in the Legion in spite of the assertion by its leaders that it is "the most democratic organization in the world" was discovered by a veteran who worked in the Legion for a while on some of its committees and, later, after its distasteful performances had forced him to quit, wrote a book called *The Inside Story of the Legion*. It is a revealing work. On the organization's totalitarian aspect, Justin Gray wrote:

> Indeed, the more I attempted to study this democracy, the less I could find of it in actual operation. Instead I found, operating behind an elaborate façade of democracy, the two

[3] William Gellermann, *The American Legion as Educator*, New York: Bureau of Publications, Teachers College, Columbia University, 1938, p. 242.

[4] Marcus Duffield, *King Legion*, New York: Jonathan Cape and Harrison Smith, 1931, chap. III, p. 33, *passim*.

factors essential to a dictatorship: a strong executive and a technique for thwarting any dissent from below.[5]

Gray describes the Legion's National Executive Committee which functions between conventions and with which the individual Legionnaire has no contact. It can, Gray says, actually reverse convention resolutions.

On the negative side, [he continues] the Legion has all kinds of techniques for suppressing dissidents or for channeling criticism, no matter how constructive, into non-constructive channels. Sometimes the technique is brutally direct, such as the ruling, fixed by Legion custom as well as law, that posts shall never publicly express opinions except through Legion "channels." In 1946, the National Executive Committee went even further, barring the individual Legionnaire from petitioning Congress, or appearing before it "in connection with any legislative matters in behalf of the Legion" except through the Legion's National Executive Committee.[6]

The *New York Herald Tribune* passed judgment on this kind of censorship in an editorial printed May 21, 1946:

It seems very late in the day to argue this simple question of independent thinking and free speech. As far back as 1934, the rules of the Legion which purported to impose this censorship were held "unreasonable and unlawful" by the New York Supreme Court. Their absurdity in a democracy is patent. But, more important, here is an effort by the Legion to perpetuate in the present a type of totalitarianism which is particularly offensive to the new veterans.

2

The American Legion was born at the beginning of the Red Scare which followed the first World War. It was presented,

[5] Justin Gray with Victor H. Bernstein, *The Inside Story of the Legion,* New York: Boni & Gaer, 1948, p. 166.
[6] *Ibid.,* pp. 174, 175.

therefore, with a new enemy that it might fight with the same ardor as a minority of its members had fought against Germany. Bolshevism was, however, a more convenient foe; it was not necessary to go overseas to gain contact with it. Bolshevism, it turned out, was right on our doorstep, in the very communities to which the soldiers, upon discharge, went home. If no real Bolshevist appeared on the threshold, it was probable that someone would soon come along to play the role albeit unwittingly. To hasten this probability the term "red" was extended to cover socialists (bitter enemies of communism), pacifists, liberals, and others who adhered to the principles in the Bill of Rights, opponents of the police measures by which such persons were persecuted, and, eventually, opponents of universal draft legislation in time of peace. The elasticity of the definition of "red" is best demonstrated by the fact that both the clergy and atheists are liable to attack: clergymen because they are generally against war; atheists because Communists are also atheists, therefore, by a false generalization, all atheists are Communists.[7]

Up to the close of 1920 fifty acts of violence by the Legion have been recorded. These aroused such criticism including that of Legionnaires themselves that other methods were subsequently resorted to. In 1921, however, at Great Bend, Kansas, four speakers at a Farmers Non-Partisan League were beaten up —two of them tarred and feathered.[8] At Wilkes-Barre in 1924 a Lenin memorial meeting was broken up at gun point.

The foreign war thus fortuitously turned into a civil one. On one side were the many patriotic organizations, some of them bred in the fringe of combat by the soldiers who had been able to keep their uniforms spotless, others created by civilian patriots. These were, in the early days, the Daughters of the American Revolution, Key Men of America, The American Coalition, the

[7] Leroy F. Smith and E. B. Johns, *Pastors, Politicians, Pacifists,* Chicago: Constructive Educational Publishing Co., 1927, *passim.*

[8] Norman Hapgood (ed.), *Professional Patriots,* New York: A. & C. Boni, 1927, p. 58.

Better America Association, the Reserve Officers Association, the Military Intelligence Association, and the Military Order of the World War. On the other side, subject to recurrent attack, were the Foreign Policy Association, the National Council for Prevention of War, the Women's International League for Peace and Freedom, the Civil Liberties Union, and the Federal Council of the Churches of Christ in America. On both sides were lesser organizations which engaged in occasional skirmishes. It was the American Legion, however, which led the more spectacular offensives.

One reason for the Legion's initial prestige was that, in the early fall of 1919, it received a charter from Congress.[9] Judging by the preamble to its Constitution, this act of incorporation was entirely proper.

> For God and country [stated this "masterpiece of the English language," as a Legion commander called it] we associate ourselves together for the following purposes: To uphold and defend the Constitution of the United States of America; to maintain law and order; to foster and perpetuate a one hundred per cent Americanism; to preserve the memories and incidents of our association in the great war . . . to promote peace and good will on earth. . . .[1]

The Legion's most dynamic activity in the early years was the upholding of the Constitution by stopping speeches. It is true that here it had the support of many communities which it was able to inoculate with the germs of fear. In the resultant panic, not only the Constitution of the United States but law and order as well were easily forgotten.

In 1926, the Legion attempted the arrest, through Indianapolis police, of Frederick J. Libby, executive secretary of the National

[9] 41 U.S. Statutes at Large, 284.
[1] 58 CR 4992.

Council for the Prevention of War, because he was scheduled to address the Indiana Council of International Relations. The police, however, seeing many important citizens at the meeting, withdrew. Thwarted in this, the Legion finally got Libby four years later by forcing the cancellation of his scheduled address to the State College at Santa Barbara, California. In the same year, it intimidated a men's club of Evanston, Illinois, into canceling an address by Dr. Karl Borders, a Chicago settlement worker.[2] In 1927, Mrs. Lucia Ames Mead, an ardent peace advocate, was vigorously opposed in her speaking tour by a coalition of patriotic societies including the Legion and, although she was able to defy their attacks as far as the state of Georgia, the Legion finally caught up with her in Atlanta and forced the cancellation of her speeches there. Soon after, the Legion engineered the cancellation of an address by Roger N. Baldwin, director of the Civil Liberties Union, before the Los Angeles City Club.[3]

A peace advocate, Sherwood Eddy, on a speaking tour in the South, had three speaking dates canceled at the instigation of the American Legion. It turned out that the Legion had informed itself of every engagement on Mr. Eddy's tour and written warning letters to the organizations that had engaged him. The Legion's Commander is quoted by Mr. Eddy as saying he would like to see him "silenced in peacetime and shot in time of war." In most cases the warnings were ignored but strenuous efforts were made to cause cancellation at every point. Other patriotic societies accused this sincere missionary of being "supported by Moscow gold."[4]

In 1931, a Legion meeting was addressed by a speaker who protested against the landing in California of Albert Einstein, described as "a pacifist travelling in the guise of a mathematician." Einstein was, at the time, an especial target of chauvinist

[2] Duffield, op. cit., pp. 210–11.
[3] Ibid., pp. 211–13. Hapgood, op. cit., p. 57.
[4] Sherwood Eddy, Eighty Adventurous Years, New York: Harper & Bros., 1955, p. 121.

attack; to the Legion he was not only a pacifist but an "internationalist" and an atheist as well.[5]

One might imagine that the Legion's rage against atheism would be difficult to reconcile with its attack upon the churches. Logic is not, however, a discipline to which the Executive Committee adheres. One Legionnaire, Colonel Leroy F. Smith, who belonged also to the Better America Federation, wrote a book called *Pastors, Politicians, Pacifists,* in which he berated the Federal Council of the Churches of Christ for encouragement of slackers, for propaganda for both the World Court and the League of Nations, for sympathy with the I.W.W., for communistic propaganda, for "tariff tinkering," for anti-preparedness and pro-Japanese propaganda, and for fostering the "subversive" Youth Movement.

Marcus Duffield in his book *King Legion* tells of the aggressive heckling by Legionnaires of a conference of the New England Fellowship of Youth for Peace, in the Trinity Church parish house of Concord, Massachusetts. He quotes the Boston *Sunday Globe* which reported the affair:

> Concord is an embattled village again. . . . The pacifists have been egged. A local clergyman was stoned while leaving one of the meetings. . . . Police have stood guard about the home of the chairman of the selectmen since the mob gathered one evening to boo and sing jeering songs under his windows, because the selectmen permitted the peace conference to meet in the Town Hall. . . .
>
> The war veterans, feeling themselves the custodians of the Revolutionary tradition, declare their town has been traduced by the presence of men some of whom were conscientious objectors in the World War. The vestrymen of Trinity Church and the older citizens, proud of Concord's tradition as the home of idealism and freedom in all its higher forms, feel equally that Concord has been disgraced by the attempts at denial of free speech and the persecution of her guests.[6]

[5] Duffield, *op. cit.,* p. 218.
[6] *Ibid.,* pp. 228, 229.

69

While it is not recorded that the egg-throwing was an official Legion performance, there was a demonstration definitely led by the Legion in the Concord town hall in which the peace group's policy was said by one of the patriot rabble-rousers "to endanger the government of the United States."[7] It is unlikely that inflamed Legionnaires would leave such a rally in a peaceable mood.

Whether the rewriting of history in the Soviet Union was inspired by the American Legion's efforts in that direction, there is a striking similarity in the two enterprises. The difference between their operation, however, is due to the fact that the Soviet Union is a totalitarian dictatorship whereas the United States is a democracy in which, despite Legion efforts to the contrary, the people have remained sovereign. It is for this reason that despite occasional conniving between the Legion and various boards of education by which textbooks were banned and teachers fired, American historians have continued to be more interested in truth than in nationalism. Their failure, here, has remained a thorn in the flesh of the American Legion as it has in that of the other patriotic societies which march in America's Sixth Column.

The result of the strong-arm methods of so many of the patriotic societies is that the opposition to some of their extremely debatable tenets has been greatly strengthened. One issue which has admitted of much discussion has been that of preparedness for war. Military disasters running all the way from Bunker Hill to the Kasserine Pass have warned us, throughout our history, of the dangers of unreadiness for battle. Many former pacifists have become convinced of the necessity of armament, yet others have been so outraged by being grouped with radicals that their pacifism has reached extremes. In any case, the right to express one's views on this as on all other subjects is constitutionally guaranteed.

In the atomic age, of course, the issue of war or peace has become largely academic.

[7] *Ibid.*, p. 229.

3

When the second World War came within the lifetimes of the first war's heroes the Legion saw an opportunity to enlarge its membership greatly. In its initial drives it did add many ex-G.I.'s though a good proportion of these did not stick. But the Legion, in 1945 and after, had some formidable competition which it had not encountered after the first World War. There were newcomers in the field, such as Charles Bolte's American Veterans Committee, whose members regarded the Legion's activities and policies as outmoded or adolescent. Most veterans of the second World War were heartily sick of war; they preferred to forget it; they saw no reason to keep alive the distasteful memories. They had known little flag-waving in their experience and less bandplaying; like European soldiers, they looked on war as a necessary but grim business in which good times were few and far between. Though half the age of the old Legionnaires they were far more mature. The bulk of them had lived their childhood in the Depression and by the time war came to America in 1941, their kit bag could not hold all their troubles.

Also, despite the efforts of the Legion and other eagle-screaming groups to arrest its development, the American people as a whole had grown more mature. It had lived through hard and perilous times. In the first months of the Pacific conflict, there was reason to believe that the United States was about to suffer the first defeat in its history and, to avert it, the people had made sacrifices unprecedented in this land of Manifest Destiny. Then, at the end, the mushroom clouds at Hiroshima and Nagasaki had, for many Americans, cast a shadow over the joy of victory.

Unhappily, the people were still vulnerable to hysterical waves of fear and this, some five years after war's end, gave the Legion one more field day. However, the old tune which its hand organ had ground out since 1920 was changed. When American armies went to the aid of South Korea in its resistance to Communist aggression, no war whoop was uttered in the Legion's convention in the autumn of 1950. Instead, this society of super-patriots turned against the government which had "got us into it" and

71

declaimed against Secretary of State Acheson and others. Speaking of this in a Columbus Day broadcast, the late Elmer Davis said:

> When the State Department has succeeded in getting almost all the world to support us in Korea, when it stands on the verge of the greatest success American diplomacy has achieved in many years—obtaining the reorganization of the United Nations so that it can act in any future crisis—just then the American Legion demands that the men who have accomplished this be fired as unable to deal with communism. If there is any better way to discourage nations that are inclined to support us I don't know what it is. Such a resolution would be understandable from the Eighth Ward Political Club three weeks before election; but it is somewhat surprising from the national convention of a patriotic organization.[8]

At the same convention the Legion, caught by this time in the first spasm of what was to become McCarthyist hysteria, resolved that all Communist Party members should be immediately interned and tried for treason. In suggesting that such a performance might not accord with provisions of the Constitution, Davis said:

> It may be argued that the Founding fathers never foresaw such an institution as the Communist party; but they probably never foresaw such an institution as the Legion's Americanism Committee either.[9]

Apologists for the Legion maintained that its unwise acts are balanced by the community services, disaster relief, co-operation with the Red Cross and other public benefits for which the organization is celebrated. It is true that rank and file Legionnaires and their families who belong to the Legion's Auxiliary enter

[8] Oct. 12, 1950, American Broadcasting Company. Roger Burlingame, *Don't Let Them Scare You: The Life and Times of Elmer Davis*, Philadelphia: J. B. Lippincott Co., 1961, p. 305.

[9] *Ibid.*, p. 306.

zealously and selflessly into these enterprises. They were designed, however, by the commanders and committees to enlist community support and, above all, to attract new members.[1] In this endeavor they have been almost uniformly successful.

4

Though the men of the Legion were earnest workers in the cause of one hundred per cent Americanism they soon needed a more ferocious inspiration. When, therefore, the assistance of the wives, sisters, mothers, and daughters of the veterans was offered, the Legion welcomed it.

American women have often formed the flying wedge in front of many historic movements. Largely through their ferocity, national prohibition became law; but the women were equally frenzied in their agitation for the repeal of the prohibition amendment. All logic was on their side in their demand for the vote but the suffragists believed that only by acts of violence could they work their will. Women have long been in the van of the peace movement but the Legion soon found that women could also be as chauvinistic as men.

At the third National Convention in 1921, those women who had accompanied their husbands got together and formed the American Legion Auxiliary. In ten years, the membership of the Auxiliary had increased to 400,000. During those ten years, the women's department closely followed the policies and program dictated by the Legion's National Executive Committee. The rank and file followed along, as unable as the rank and file of the men to exert any influence whatever on the directions in which the Auxiliary went. They did, however, make contributions of a social nature, organizing parties to celebrate events in the Legion's progress, arranging recreational programs and teaching the children of Legionnaires to become one hundred per cent patriots. To the life and welfare of many communities they became increasingly important. In the Auxiliary, the same distinc-

[1] Duffield, *op. cit.*, p. 21.

73

tion could be made between the decent, democratic, well-intentioned members who formed the bulk of the society and the small dictatorial pressure group at the top.

The Auxiliary had the advantage of affiliation with some of the fiercest female leagues in the nation, and therefore, in the world. Within a few years of their founding they had organized an annual conference attended by delegates from the Daughters of the American Revolution, the Daughters of Colonial Wars, the Colonial Daughters, Daughters of the Seventeenth Century, Daughters of the Defenders of the Republic, Daughters of the Cincinnati, Daughters of 1812, Daughters of Founders and Patriots, Daughters of Union Veterans of the Civil War, United Daughters of the Confederacy and others—altogether thirty-eight female societies, all savage in their determination to save the country from its subversives.

Normally we think of women as being dedicated to peace. In all history the women have mourned their soldier dead and declaimed about the brutality of war which took their men from them. But not these ladies. To them an advocate of peace was *ipso facto* a Bolshevist, an "internationalist" (and therefore un-American) or, most hated of all, a "liberal." They did, to be sure, explain their jingoism by plugging for "preparedness" as a deterrent but they gained great favor, nonetheless, with the militarists of the Army and the Navy, several of whom addressed the conference.

At one conference, the chairman of the D.A.R.'s National Defense Committee made a spirited speech about the similarities between pacifism, socialism and communism.

I see [said Mrs. William Sherman Walker] the Soviet plan working everywhere in America. I see people quarrelling over things they do not understand, babbling of peace that means only weakness and death. . . . Pacifists prepare letters for signature by housewives and busy people who have not time to write letters of their own accord. They ring doorbells and beg busy people to sign these letters as a token of their desire

74

for world peace. Unsuspecting any unusual motive, thousands of signatures are obtained in this way from guileless people.[2]

The unsuspected "motive," is, of course, to weaken the United States to a point at which the Soviets can take over. This outrageous charge was buttressed by brochures and pamphlets giving details and naming names. Some of the names listed in one pamphlet were Nicholas Murray Butler, President of Columbia University, Reeve Schley, vice-president of the Chase National Bank, Henry Ford, John Dewey, and Owen D. Young. The accusations included tolerance toward revolutionary communism, business dealings with Russia, radical propaganda, and "internationalist activities."

The large membership of the Auxiliary is as useful to the Legion's legislative lobby as is that of the Legion itself. When any piece of lawmaking is especially desired by the Legislative Committee, telegrams are sent to the women as to the men, urging them to write or wire their representatives and senators. This demand is refused by those women who object to being stampeded as it often is by the more thoughtful Legionnaires but a goodly proportion accedes through fear of being "disloyal" to the Legion. In the conflict of loyalties among both sexes the Legion frequently wins out over "God and country."

5

To these branches of the Sixth Column there is, as to the others, plenty of healthy opposition. In recent years in which labor has found new freedoms and new tolerance of its rights; in which awareness has increased of the necessity of collective security among nations; in which the physical isolation has vanished; in which there appears no defense against nuclear attack, and in which American prestige in the world scene has sunk to an all-time low—the patriotic societies have lost much of their appeal. And since most Americans are veterans of some sort, the halo that once hung over a veteran's head has lost its lustre, so that a

[2] *Ibid.*, p. 245.

veteran's organization, today, is almost a committee of the whole. Even the young men who can hardly remember a hot war have had experiences in the draft which tend to dim illusions of glory, and spinal chills of patriotism are rarely induced in them even by the most spirited Sousa marches.

In the lowered temperatures of the cold war, the American Legion has been criticized along with a number of other formerly sacrosanct groups. Articles, editorials, and books have exposed the stupid ignorance of its name-calling and its empty arrogance but, most of all, its totalitarian structure. Even in the Congress whose members once followed like sheep after the Legion's bellwether, there is now, outside the Un-American Activities Committee in the House and its opposite number in the Senate, outspoken opposition.

An especially forthright book, meticulously documented, is William Gellermann's *The American Legion in Education*. The "Conclusions" of this study show that the Legion's influence is due to a pressure group within a pressure group. They show that most of the Legion's huge membership are dupes of the extremely small body of policy-makers at its top, yet the whole acts like a bulldozer in carrying out the will of its operator. Thus a highly conscious pressure-group works upon a largely unconscious body to cause it to exert its pressure upon the Congress, the Government, and the people.[3]

Since some of its teeth have been pulled by changing circumstance, it may be supposed that the American Legion is no longer dangerous as an instrument of the Sixth Column. But, though its methods have become more subtle, it is no less a threat to traditional American freedoms. In its clandestine support to the witch-hunting committees of the Congress it can be more venomous and less vulnerable.

[3] Gellermann, *op. cit.*, p. 241. The whole of chap. IX, pp. 238–66, is instructive.

V. Un-American

BEFORE COMING to the establishment of the House Un-American Activities Committee as a "standing" committee in 1945—an act which made it a permanent branch of the American Sixth Column—it is instructive to examine the precedents given it by Martin Dies who has been charged with making his experimental group acting from 1938 to 1944 a "one man committee."

Dies was a Texas Democrat who followed his father in the House of Representatives and, like the elder Dies, was known for paradoxical and sometimes eccentric behavior. His contradictory conduct in the political area does not, however, seem so strange when we realize that even in the 1930's the southern Democrats were often more aligned with the Republicans than with their own party in the North. Martin Dies, the younger, became a special darling of the Republicans, if not from the moment of his election to the House, certainly after he became chairman of what was universally known as the Dies Committee. And well he might be, for he began at once to engineer, through his committee, the election of Republicans to replace Democrats in the legislative body. Furthermore, as he developed the unconstitutional techniques of his committee he incurred the hostility of President Roosevelt and, in return, allowed his henchmen to carry their smears into the Roosevelt household and their character assassination into the Cabinet.[1]

Within a year of the balanced speeches with which he had

[1] William Gellermann, *Martin Dies,* New York: John Day Co., 1944, *passim.*

77

argued, in May, 1938, in favor of the resolution creating his committee, Martin Dies had gone into complete reverse. "Neither the public nor Congress," he had said, "will have any confidence in the findings of a committee which adopts a partisan or a preconceived attitude. Statements and charges unsupported by facts have no evidentiary value and only tend to confuse the issue. It is easy to 'smear' someone's name or reputation by unsupported charges or an unjustified attack, but it is difficult to repair the damage that has been done."

In the summer and autumn of 1938, Dies forgot his caution against partisanship by using his committee to discredit the New Deal's programs as communistic. This was a boon to Republican candidates in the election campaign and resulted in criticism of the committee by the President. Immediately after this, two Democrat members of his own committee sent Dies this telegram:

> We are greatly disturbed by the charges made yesterday by the President himself that procedure has been adopted which has permitted the committee to be improperly used for election purposes, and we particularly deplore the kind of attack that has been permitted upon an outstanding Government servant like Governor Murphy of Michigan.[2]

One of these committee members later pointed out that Martin Dies had also forgotten his eloquent words about "smearing" with unsupported charges. A letter to Dies from committeeman John J. Dempsey stated:

> I know of nothing more cowardly than to permit wild and irrational statements which have no basis in fact and have only for their end the assassination of characters of men who are outstanding and whom both you and I know to be American citizens of the highest type. . . . If we are to expect such a continuation I have no other alternative than to ask the Speaker of the House to accept my resignation as a mem-

[2] 83 CR 1110.

ber of the committee and to insist that my name be used no further in connection with the committee's activities.[3]

From a colleague these are strong words. They show how widely Congressman Dies had deviated from his earlier sentiments—granting, of course, that those *were* his sentiments and not *ad hoc* eloquence for the purpose of getting his resolution adopted without objection from those members of the House who understood the function of investigating committees. At least one representative whom Dies had convinced of his sincerity in May, 1938, was shocked by the changes that had taken place by February, 1939, when a resolution was presented to continue the Un-American Activities Committee.

Mr. Speaker [said Adolph J. Sabath, Democrat from Illinois, Chairman of the House Rules Committee] I supported and voted for the resolution that created this special committee in the belief that I was helping to bring about a real investigation of all the un-American and subversive activities in the country. I was therefore amazed to find out during the course of the hearings before the Committee on Rules that little or none of the original intent of the House had been carried out. Instead I became convinced that the committee had spent its time and money in little less than a "smearing campaign" against all who have tried to promote liberal government and aid in supporting the great humanitarian principles of your President and mine.[4]

2

The public hearings of the Dies Committee had opened with the testimony of a witness, John P. Frey[5] that the Congress of Industrial Organizations was "Moscow dominated" and that many of the CIO's leaders were Communists, statements that aroused much sensational publicity and had exceedingly dam-

[3] *Ibid.*
[4] *Ibid.*, 1102.
[5] Hearings before a Special Committee on Un-American Activities, 75th Cong., 3d Sess., vol. 1, pp. 91*ff*, Aug. 13, 15, 16, 1938.

aging effects. No doubt it was the press response to this attack that changed the tone of Dies's thinking, for this congressman delighted in lurid headlines. As Kenneth G. Crawford comments in his book *The Pressure Boys: The Inside Story of Lobbying in America* (New York: 1939):

It was probably the amazing success of the Frey testimony as an experiment in publicity that awakened Dies and his associates to a full realization of the potentialities of the political gold mine that they had struck. From then on it was catch as catch can with no holds barred.[6]

The Frey sensation was followed by the testimony of Walter S. Steele, a professional patriot,[7] who said he was chairman of the National Security Committee of the American Coalition of Patriotic, Civic and Fraternal Societies—a group of one hundred and fourteen organizations among which were the American War Mothers, the Colonial Order of the Acorn, the Dames of the Loyal Legion of the United States, the National Council of the Patriotic Women of America, Inc., and The Wheel of Progress. Steele contributed a list of 640 organizations which he said were not only "communistic" but "dangerously inter-nationalist." Among these were the Boy Scouts, the Camp Fire Girls, and the Catholic Association for International Peace. He also brought charges against thousands of individuals. With the later testimony of J. B. Matthews before the committee doubt was cast on the intelligence if not the loyalty of America's darling of the movies, Shirley Temple. She had, it seems, endorsed a French newspaper, said to be Communist. This aroused ridicule outside the humorless ranks of the Sixth Column when various newspapers became skeptical of Miss Temple's power, talented actress though she was, to overthrow the government by force or violence.

[6] Kenneth G. Crawford, *The Pressure Boys: The Inside Story of Lobbying in America*, New York: Julian Messner, Inc., 1939, p. 112.

[7] Hearings before Special Committee on Un-American Activities, 75th Cong., 3d Sess., vol. 1, pp. 278*ff*, Aug. 16, 1938.

After the Special Committee to investigate Un-American Activities had submitted, in January, 1939, its first report telling the House of all these devastating triumphs, Martin Dies introduced a resolution for his committee's continuance. In the debate over this, Representative Sabath, not only expressed dismay that the committee had not kept its chairman's promises but also said that, as head of the Rules Committee, he had been flooded with letters and telegrams objecting to Dies and his methods. He submitted thirty-seven of these from organizations and individuals.[8] They had come from the Brotherhood of Railroad Trainmen, the Indiana Civil Rights Committtee, the Friends of Democracy, Syracuse University School of Citizenship and Public Affairs, the Council for Economic and Social Research of Portland, Oregon, the South Bend Industrial Union Council, the Texas Civil Liberties Committee, Labor's Non-Partisan League of Connecticut, the Progressive Education Association, the Ohio League for Constitutional Rights, the American Federation of Teachers, the Winnetka Public Schools, the Yale University School of Law, Southern Illinois State Teachers College, the American Civil Liberties Union, the Council of United States Veterans, Inc., and others. They were all hostile or contemptuous and several demanded the abolition of the Dies Committtee.

One letter from Carleton Washburne of the Winnetka Public Schools stated what many have thought to be the answer to the whole question of Red hunts:

If there are actual criminal conspiracies, let our very efficient G-men ferret them out under the Department of Justice, instead of dragging citizens before a congressional committee to explain why they have exercised their rights as citizens in a free country in belonging to various organizations or expressing their opinions . . .

Dies investigations smack of the Stalin purges and the Hitler persecutions. They are far more un-American than the activities of those whom he exposes.[9]

[8] 83 CR, debate on resolution 1098–1129. Letters, etc., 1104–1106.
[9] *Ibid.*, 1104.

In support of this position and in argument against the resolution to continue, Representative John M. Coffee, Democrat of the State of Washington, submitted excerpts from twenty-two newspaper and magazine editorials. These included adverse expressions from *Time*, the Richmond *Times-Dispatch*, the Seattle *Daily Times*, the Minneapolis *Star*, the Tampa *Morning Tribune*, the Galveston *Daily News*, the Utica *Press*, the Waco (Tex.) *News-Tribune*, the Buffalo *Times*, the Denver *Rocky Mountain News*, and the Kansas City *Journal*.[1]

In spite of all this testimony, however, a large majority of the representatives, spurred by the bogey fears of the super-patriots, voted to continue the Dies Committee.

As the war came nearer through 1940 and 1941, Dies was accused of neglecting what were said to be Nazi conspiracies against the government, in favor of Red plots which he continued, up to the Pearl Harbor attack, to emphasize. In August, September and October, 1941, according to reports of the Federal Communications Commission's monitoring service, Dies received in Axis broadcasts to the United States "as many favorable references . . . as any living American public figure."[2] In 1942 when the Board of Economic Warfare was working overtime for the war effort, the Dies committee accused thirty-five of its members of joining Communist-front organizations, news of which was gloatingly given in three Axis propaganda broadcasts.[3]

The committee did not expire until 1944. During that time it had spent $652,500 for its expenses.[4] Its decease came because it was a "special" not a "standing" committee and, late in 1944, the House did not vote for its extension. In the following year, however, in the Seventy-ninth Congress, the House created a standing Committee on Un-American Activities which has continued to operate on the pattern laid down by Martin Dies.

[1] *Ibid.*, 1123–1126.
[2] *Facts on File*, Feb. 11, 1942.
[3] *Ibid.*, Apr. 2, 1942.
[4] Robert K. Carr, *The House Committee on Un-American Activities 1945–1950*, Ithaca: Cornell University Press, 1952, p. 17n.

3

According to Professor Robert K. Carr of Dartmouth, who has written the definitive history of the *House Committee on Un-American Activities 1945-1950*, the revival of the Dies investigating group and its new position as a "standing committee" of the House "was engineered almost singlehandedly by Representative John Rankin."[5] The deafening tones of this congressman's oratory delivered in the broadest of Mississippi accents had for many years been a familiar noise in the House; also Mr. Rankin was able to add to this benumbing technique a knowledge of parliamentary procedure that amazed and often defeated his colleagues.

By the time of its expiration in 1944, the Dies committee had become moribund; the imminence of victory in the war had taken priority in the minds of the members of Congress and the apparent fading of the Communist menace since the military alliance with Russia had diverted most Americans from the un-American pursuit. Furthermore, the decision of Martin Dies not to run for re-election in 1944 had removed Hamlet from the play. Dies had, indeed, become the committee and without him, what would be left?

Much, believed Rankin, the deep South Democrat; an Un-American Activities Committee could still be useful to Rankin's friends, the Republicans; then, too, who could tell what an epidemic of new subversion might spread in the wake of the war? Uppermost in his mind, however, was the fear that, now that the Dies committee was dead, its precious records might be destroyed, leaving none of the extensive lists of names of subversives to which future smears might be applied when desired. A new committee could take these over and keep them alive; if it were permanent, witch hunts could be resumed at any time.

Rankin, therefore, worked out tactics for jamming through a vote for an Un-American activities committee and told no one. He was thoroughly conversant with all the technical devices that

[5] *Ibid.*, p. 19. Chap. 6 of Carr's book gives a character analysis of all members of the Committee during the period 1945–1950.

would further his plan, but he knew also the value of surprise. So when the Seventy-ninth Congress opened two days after New Year's, 1945, Rankin was on his toes in the House. The action that followed close on the opening is graphically described by Professor Carr.

Hardly had the House of Representatives convened on January 3 for the brief, formal session characteristic of the first day of a new Congress when his opportunity came. The usual resolution was offered by Representative Sabath, Chairman of the Rules Committee in the previous Congress, that the rules of the House in the 78th Congress remain in effect for the new Congress. Immediately, Rankin was on his feet with an amendment to this resolution to the effect that the Un-American Activities Committee be added to the list of standing committees of the House. The cleverness of Rankin's move lay in the fact that the Sabath resolution had to be voted upon at once and could not be referred to the Rules Committee for deliberation and a recommendation, since technically no committee existed until the resolution itself was adopted. Normally, major changes in the rules of the House of Representatives or the creation of new committees are proposed in resolutions offered after a new session gets under way, in which case they must necessarily be submitted to the Rules Committee for what often proves to be prolonged consideration and ultimate pigeonholing. But the wily Rankin saw that the customary reluctance of the House to support any attempt to railroad through a change in the rules on the first day might well be overcome by the fear of House members, often indicated in the preceding years, that any kind of vote against the un-American activities investigation would be politically unwise.[6]

Nevertheless there was strong opposition. Though Speaker Rayburn explained that the conventional procedure would ensure the safekeeping of the Dies records, Rankin was insistent. Though the first division vote was against him, the record vote he called

[6] *Ibid.*, p. 20. 91 CR 10, Jan. 3, 1945.

for passed the amendment by the narrow margin of 208 to 186. In the vote for it were 137 Republicans and 70 Democrats, 63 of whom were southerners.[7] Thus, as Professor Carr points out, "it was a coalition of Republican and Southern Democrats which was responsible for the creation of a permanent Un-American Activities Committee."[8]

The language of the Rankin amendment specifying the functions of the new committee was virtually the same as the original Dies resolution of seven years before but the personnel of the standing committee was quite different. Gone were the objecting northern Democrats, Healy and Dempsey; of the six new Democrats there were three northerners, three from the South. Of the Republicans, two—J. Parnell Thomas of New Jersey and Karl E. Mundt of South Dakota—hung over from the Dies Committee of 1944. A Democrat, Edward J. Hart of New Jersey, was elected chairman.

By that time, however, it had become customary for such a committee to employ a considerable staff of outsiders including lawyers, "investigators," filing clerks, and other clerical workers. Later incidents suggested that the lawyers were chosen for their astuteness and a talent for the ruthless browbeating of witnesses (who were not permitted to be represented by counsel). The staff did most of the work of obtaining testimony.

4

Staff investigation was a full-time, year-round job. Research was carried on through regional offices. Information about individuals was obtained in the communities in which they lived. Clippings from newspapers, programs of meetings or entertainments, pamphlets, the "literature" of alleged subversive organizations were assiduously collected and sent to Washington where they were kept in the committee's central files. Lists of individual names were also compiled without appraisal or evaluation, those of wholly innocent citizens lumped together with Commu-

[7] *Ibid.*, p. 14.
[8] Carr, *op. cit.*, p. 23.

nist Party members and authentic radical conspirators. One of the committee's chiefs of staff once boasted that a million names were thus filed.

In theory, the material contained in the committee's two hundred file cabinets is restricted. Access to the files is not granted to everyone who requests it. It is granted, however, to so many persons that the information the collection contains can hardly be said to be confidential. The files are open, for example, to Congressmen and to the staffs of congressional committees. They may also be consulted by government officials connected with agencies concerned with loyalty and security. A staff boast has estimated that the files have been used by twenty thousand persons.[9] The chairman of the standing committee in 1947 stated that in the first five months of that year, the files were visited by 512 persons, who checked 8,529 names.[1] From so large a body, leaks into many private channels are inevitable. It is probable that any persevering executive who wants to check on a prospective employee will have little difficulty in discovering whether or not there is a dossier on the person's past.

The availability of these lists and dossiers to members of Congress has sometimes furnished campaign material to those who are running for re-election.[2] If the name of the opponent is listed in the files, however vaguely, the Congressman can easily suggest to the voters in his district that his rival has engaged in "un-American" conduct. The opponent, having no access to the files, is therefore at a disadvantage. He can produce no proof that his listing is unwarranted or accidental; he has no means of defending himself against charges which may be wholly irresponsible.

The "research" into the un-American behavior of individuals and organizations is carried on by the investigators with the aid of local chapters of various patriotic associations. The American Legion has been of frequent assistance in the branding of "sub-

[9] *Ibid.,* p. 256.
[1] 93 CRA 2546, May 29, 1947.
[2] Carr, *op. cit.,* pp. 256f. 92 CRA 4942, Aug. 2, 1946.

versives" who may merely be "internationalists" or peace advocates. Another is the notorious American Business Consultants, Inc., organized by former agents of the FBI, which has published the weekly "newsletter" *Counterattack* since May, 1947, and, in 1950 the booklet *Red Channels*,[3] a listing of subversives for the use of radio and television executives. The most cursory glance at this little book shows that its compilers, an independent business organization not in any way connected with government, have had unrestrained access to the files of the House Un-American Activities Committee. Nearly every person listed has been cited by the committee. Others that have collaborated with the committee's far-flung staff agents are the Veterans of Foreign Wars, AWARE, Inc., the Christian Anti-Communist Crusade and the Daughters of the American Revolution. This affiliation has been called "the Network" by Frank J. Donner in his book *The Un-Americans*.[4] It furnishes an elaborate mechanism for the exposure function of the committee and it gives the committee enough advance information about the witnesses the committee will call to enable it to rig its hearings. This machinery thus effectively nullified the pious statement made by Martin Dies in 1938: "The committee has no preconceived views of what the truth is respecting the subject matter of this inquiry." The fact is that from 1945 no hearing was ever conducted without preconceived views regarding the witness being arrived at through extensive exploration by the staff.

One of the staff's main duties was the separation of the sheep from the goats among witnesses subpoenaed by the committee: friendly and unfriendly witnesses having been designated in those terms by the staff investigators. A "friendly" witness was one who was as dedicated to the witch hunt as the committee itself; an "unfriendly" witness was one who might resist the committee's

[3] *Red Channels, the Report of Communist Influence in Radio and Television,* published by *Counterattack, The Newsletter of Facts to Combat Communism,* 55 West 42d Street, New York 18, N.Y.

[4] Frank J. Donner, *The Un-Americans,* New York: Ballantine Books, 1961, chap. 4.

87

bullying and try to stand on the rights guaranteed him by the Constitution. By employing a staff, the committee was able to shift the responsibility of robbing a citizen of the privileges to which his citizenship entitled him. Several members of the committee were, at times, exceedingly reluctant to pursue such high-pressure tactics in the examination of witnesses and they were glad to have the staff relieve them of the guilt.

Though no witness was ever permitted to have himself represented by counsel as he would have done in any court of law, he was allowed to have an attorney accompany him with whom he might consult before answering questions. After the committee's techniques became known, however, to the legal profession generally, witnesses were advised by their counsel to decline to answer certain questions on the grounds that their answers might incriminate them.[5] This falling back on the Fifth Amendment to the Constitution, which provides that no one shall be compelled to be a witness against himself, proved very embarrassing to the committee in many instances and it has created the angriest controversy of all.

Counsel had advised witnesses to invoke the privilege of the Fifth Amendment because of a legal technicality known as the "doctrine of waiver." This provides that once a witness has voluntarily answered certain questions, he automatically waives his right to refuse to answer later related questions. He has, the courts hold, voluntarily opened up a "field of inquiry" which he then has no right to close by a pleading of constitutional privilege. Thus if a man says "No" to what is jocosely termed the "sixty-four dollar question": "Are you now or have you ever been a member of the Communist Party?," he may not plead the Fifth Amendment when he is asked to disclose the names of Communists he may know, or any other question relating to Communist Party membership. The United States Supreme Court made this clear by stating in the *Rogers* v. *U.S.* case in 1951, "Dis-

[5] Dan Gillmor, *Fear, the Accuser,* New York: Abelard-Schuman, Ltd., 1954, chap. 12.

closure of a fact waives the privilege as to details,"[6] and the Supreme Court of Michigan in *Foster* v. *People* as far back as 1869:

Where a witness has voluntarily answered as to materially criminating facts, it is held with uniformity that he cannot then stop short and refuse further explanation, but must disclose fully what he has attempted to relate.[7]

Counsel has therefore advised clients to plead the Fifth Amendment against self-incrimination at the very start of questioning lest they be later caught by the waiver doctrine. And unscrupulous staff investigators have deliberately tried to trick "unfriendly" witnesses in a committee hearing into laying themselves open to a citation of "contempt of Congress." Where a witness is so cited by the House or Senate, he is turned over to the courts for prosecution and punishment. An attorney naturally wants to keep his client out of jail for mistakenly relying on this constitutional guarantee.

Though committees have usually accepted the Fifth Amendment plea when properly used, they have, through the staff's "network," managed to give such damaging publicity to the pleader that he has often lost his job and become unemployable. With the co-operation of local newspapers and suspicious employers, committees have caused many such losses to those they wished to expose as "subversive characters." This technique reached its peak when the late Senator McCarthy coined the term "Fifth-Amendment Communists."

Through the years of the Dies Committee and the first years of the standing House Committee to Investigate Un-American Activities (commonly known as HUAC) there has been a progressive perversion of the traditional purposes and rationale of Congressional investigating committees. Many such committees have,

[6] Rogers v. U.S., 340 U.S. 367, 373 (1951).
[7] Foster v. People, 18 Michigan 266, 276. Both the Rogers and Foster cases are cited in Telford Taylor, *Grand Inquest, the Story of Congressional Investigations*, Ballantine edition, New York: Ballantine Books, 1961, p. 224 and notes.

in the past, been extremely useful, and, indeed, necessary to the proper legislative functions of Congress. But they have been strictly limited by custom and law to inquiries that would aid legislation, not instruments of exposure for its own sake or bodies with punitive powers. Since the focus on communism, subversion, and un-American conduct, whatever that may mean, investigating committees have expanded their activities into the realm reserved by the Constitution to the courts; they have subjected citizens to court procedures while depriving them of court protection; they have caused the infliction of severe, sometimes fatal, punishment to innocent persons; and they have spread an epidemic of fear that, in braver times, would have been wholly un-American.[8]

In the exposure of alleged subversion, the investigating committees of the Congress have adopted a single principle: in every case *the end attained justifies the means of attaining it.*

[8] Taylor, *op. cit.*, Preface.

VI. Betrayal of Academic Freedom

THE PRIMARY CAUSE of the American climate of fear is ignorance. In certain directions our education is dangerously defective. The Sixth Column uses elaborate devices to make it more so.

Every group we have reviewed has had a hand in retarding education: the House Un-American Activities Committee, the American Legion, and the other "patriotic" societies. To these may be added the Internal Security Committee of the Senate and two of its subcommittees, and most recently the John Birch Society.

One reason why some of these organizations have worked so hard to interrupt American education is that their members are so profoundly ignorant themselves and are anxious to keep the people down to their level of learning. If an occasional member knows better, he dares not say so: first, because it would disturb the unified thought of his organization, and second, because if the people knew what he does, they would lose their fear and there would no longer be a reason for the organization's activity.

Most prevalent is ignorance of the nature of communism. It is this ignorance that makes the congressional investigating committees, the American Legion, and especially the John Birch Society so communistic. In their avowed fight against what they thought was communism, they have adopted all the techniques of true communism: strong-arm suppression of speech, press, teaching, and assembly; attack against non-conformity of thought, not infrequently resulting in the putting of innocent persons in prison; and the attempt to turn our once free nation into a police state.

91

These are the most repugnant practices of Communist Russia and her satellites and of Communist China. These are even more disastrous in their effect upon society than the practices that follow communism's economic philosophy—state ownership of property and enterprise.

The members of the Sixth Column, however, are concerned only with the economic philosophy because that seeks to undermine our so-called free enterprise and hence is the number one fear-making factor. Because they do know, vaguely, about this, they lump communism, socialism, and anarchy together and believe them to have equal value as menaces. The other isms which were once confused with communism—pacifism and internationalism—have lately been largely eliminated from the Sixth Column enemy by changing circumstance and certain military instruction.

It is the basic difference of concept that makes the Socialist Party so hated by the true Communist. Both believe, to be sure, in some form of nationalization of property and business. Both believe that there must be revolution of a sort to replace capitalism with this system. But the radical difference between the Communist and the Socialist is that the Communist believes this revolution must be violent and won by force, whereas the Socialist wishes to achieve it by constitutional means at the polls. To the Socialist, violent overthrow of a government is anathema. Thus the Socialists are no more of a menace than the Republicans or, indeed, the Democrats (with whom, to be sure, they are frequently confused, especially in Congress).

The anarchists, who are few in number, favor the total abolition of government, a view obviously distasteful to nations behind the iron and bamboo curtains.

We may now see why the Communists regard the Sixth Column so favorably. They are pleasantly aware that this prevailing confusion effectively prevents the Sixth Column from concentrating its fire upon communism. The Communists are further watching with mounting eagerness the steady deterioration of the strength the United States derives from its Constitution, its liberties, its democracy, and its guarantees of the rights and dignity of individual citizens. They naturally delight in the strenuous efforts of the House Un-American Activities Committee, the various Senate investigating committees, the American Legion, and, lately, the John Birch Society to destroy that precious and necessary strength.

The Russians themselves have testified to the benefits communism has gained through the ignorant anti-Communist activities in the United States. In the Russian-language *Literary Gazette* of Moscow on April 4, 1961, an article appeared declaring that

The predictions of Lenin are materializing in the course of history. Lenin predicted that the capitalistic society will strangle itself to death due to their economic and social system. This is exactly the way Lenin's predictions are coming true in the United States of America.

Lenin said that the most ardent foes of Communism will eventually become frightened and suspicious of anybody that does not agree with them. In this manner these extremely nationalistic capitalists will actually work for the cause of communism by eliminating some of the largest obstacles on the road toward a world wide communist way of life.

This was true in the past and history is repeating itself again. Several years ago an American Senator by the name of McCarthy performed a great service to world Communism and actually supported our cause by throwing suspicion of Communist affiliation on some very important personalities of the Capitalist world. He was so involved in this particular activity that instead of harming he actually strengthened the Communist party in the USA.

Now the Communist movement has gained unexpectedly a new supporter. His name is Robert Welch. . . .

According to Welch, John Foster Dulles was a Communist agent, and his brother Allen Dulles, the child of American Intelligence, is, after Eisenhower, the second largest supporter of Communism in Washington. Eisenhower's brother, Milton, is actually the boss of the American Communist Party. . . .

This is the teaching of Robert Welch and his John Birch Society. Here is more proof that Lenin's teachings and predictions were correct.[1]

A study of communism, its philosophy, its political origins, and its history by the members of the Senate and House committees engaged in investigating un-American activities and by the top officials of the American Legion would have prevented the blunders by which these agents gave, and continue to give, aid and comfort to the enemy they are spending so much effort, time, and money trying to oppose. But not only did these members of the Sixth Column not make such a study; they also did everything possible to prevent such a study being made by any American student. In this they were not quite successful, but they did obstruct the education of a considerable part of the American people in these necessary directions.

2

As we have seen, the American Legion was a pioneer in the attack on American education. It began its offensive soon after the first World War. This organization whose membership has varied through the years from somewhat less to somewhat more than a million is very largely composed of decent American citizens who have served at one time or another in the armed forces. But, almost from the beginning, it has been run from the top by a gang as ignorant, as bigoted, and as arrogant as any that has ever controlled a supposedly patriotic group of Americans.

The return to "normalcy" after World War I produced a firebrand named Charles Grant Miller who, in the employ of William Randolph Hearst, conducted a hot campaign for the suppression of "unpatriotic" textbooks in the schools. Not yet, in the

[1] Quoted in report on John Birch Society to Governor Edmund G. Brown of California by Stanley Mosk, Attorney-General, and Howard H. Jewel, Assistant Attorney-General of California, July 7, 1961, pp. 10, 11. Translated for commentator William Winter, American Broadcasting Co.

early 1920's, convinced that the American Revolution had ended, he condemned as "pro-British" eight books of American history in use in New York City schools. He went on to ferret out other subversive books: among them, the histories of Albert Bushnell Hart, Edwin Greenlaw, William West, A. C. McLaughlin, and Claude Van Tyne. In this campaign he was supported by the American Legion and nine other societies of professional patriots. Although the Legion's Americanism Commission, which investigated the subversion, did not go as far in fanaticism as Miller, the Legion adopted his thesis that the best American history was American propaganda. Textbooks, the Legion believed, should be selective, emphasizing heroic, patriotic, and militarily successful deeds and subduing the errors. Historians were criticized in an official Legion statement for "placing before immature pupils the blunders, mistakes and frailties of prominent heroes and patriots of our nation. History lays the foundation for future citizenship to a great extent and it should contain inspiration and good example for the boys and girls, inspiriting love of country and admiration for noble ideals. . . ."

This infallible recipe for complacency was presently used by the Legion to cook up an American history of its own. Marcus Duffield describes its publication in *King Legion*.

> *The Story of Our American People*, as the Legion's history was entitled, was issued by the United States History Publishing Company, a subsidiary of Parke, Austin and Lipscombe, a New York City firm of which Colonel Lemuel Bolles, former National Adjutant of the Legion, was vice-president. In the front of the book it is explained that the text was examined and revised by statesmen, including seven Senators, three generals, Dr. Archibald E. Stevenson, principal author of New York's famous Lusk Report [New York State's contribution to the Red Scare], Miss Etta V. Leighton, civic secretary of the National Security League, R. M. Whitney, author of *Reds in America* . . . and the chairman of both the Republican and Democratic parties.[2]

[2] Duffield, *op. cit.*, pp. 272–73.

In its 1925 National Convention, orders were issued to rank and file Legionnaires to sponsor the book's adoption throughout the country. It is to the credit of the individual members that on this rare occasion they, for the most part, declined to obey their bosses.

The unsuccess of their textbook did not, however, dampen the Legion's ardor in trying to control the curricula of the schools. Everywhere, principals were told by local posts to add a patriotism course to their already full schedules and were provided with detailed outlines on the history of the Stars and Stripes, the proper use and handling of the flag, allegiance to it including reiteration of the oath and other similar matters—the whole to extend over eighteen weeks. A good many schools were persuaded, or intimidated, into adopting the project, a somewhat exaggerated and over-sentimentalized version of the indoctrination and propaganda then beginning to be introduced into elementary education in the Soviet Union.[3]

3

Though the American Legion was a pioneer in the interference with education in the primary and secondary schools, it was not alone in the effort following the Red Scare of the 1920's. The federal government's movement to round up, arrest, and deport suspected subversives spawned local action in various states. We have seen the spasms of hysteria that occurred in the immediate post-war year in Massachusetts and Michigan; these were succeeded in New York by the notorious Lusk "investigation," a punitive expedition directed in large measure against schools, colleges, and the teachers therein.

From the Lusk committee's conclusions emerged a series of bills passed by both houses of the New York State legislature. One of these required a teacher's certificate of loyalty before he could teach in any school or college supported by public funds, such certificate to be revokable by the Commissioner "for any act

[3] *Ibid.*, pp. 276ff.

or utterance showing that he is not obedient to the constitution and laws of this state or of the United States, or that he is not desirous of the welfare of the country or that he is not *in hearty accord and sympathy with the government and institutions of this State or of the United States.*" (Emphasis added.)[4]

The second bill provided that no school or course of instruction could be established without first obtaining a license from the University of the State of New York, such license not to be granted unless the Board of Regents were "satisfied that the instruction proposed to be given will not be detrimental to public interest." This license was also revokable if the regents decided that the school's instruction was "detrimental to the public interests,"[5] a proviso so vague that it gave as much power to the granters of the license as was held by any commissar of education in the Soviet Union.

This legislation was promptly vetoed by Governor Alfred E. Smith, whose veto message is described by Lawrence H. Chamberlain in his book, *Loyalty and Legislative Action,* as "a notable document in the literature of civil liberty." The legislation's avowed purpose, the Governor wrote,

is to safeguard the institutions and traditions of the country. In effect, it strikes at the very foundation of one of the most cardinal institutions of our nation—the fundamental right of the people to enjoy full liberty in the domain of idea and speech. To this fundamental right there is and can be under our system of government but one limitation, namely, that the law of the land shall not be transgressed, and there is abundant statute law prohibiting the abuse of free speech. It is unthinkable that in a representative democracy there should be delegated to any body of men the absolute power to prohibit the teaching of any subject of which it may disapprove. . . .

The proponents of these bills urge that they are essential to the protection of the community against radical opinion. I might rest upon the saying of Benjamin Franklin that "they

[4] Chamberlain, *op. cit.,* p. 40.
[5] *Ibid.,* p. 41.

97

that can give up essential liberty to obtain a little temporary safety deserve neither liberty nor safety." But I go further— the safety of this government and its institutions rests upon the reasoned and devoted loyalty of its people. It does not need for its defense a system of intellectual tyranny which, in the endeavor to choke error by force, must of necessity crush truth as well.[6]

The Lusk laws were signed by interim Governor Nathan Miller in 1921 and remained in force till Smith's re-election in 1923,[7] after which, under Smith's persistent prodding, the legislature repealed them.

In signing these [repeal] bills, [the re-elected governor wrote] I firmly believe that I am vindicating the principle that, within the limits of the Penal Law, every citizen may speak and teach what he believes.[8]

With the erasing of these statutes, New York's Sixth Column received a setback, but it was not defeated. In succeeding state legislatures a series of investigations penetrated the public schools and tax-supported colleges, especially of New York City. These were not strictly "investigations," as each was introduced in the resolution creating it by the categorical statement that subversion existed in the schools, that they had been infiltrated by Communists, and that their curricula included the teaching of radical doctrines.

The McNaboe resolution of May, 1936, for example, contains the following:

WHEREAS, Our students are daily exposed to seditious or treasonable utterances in literature openly circulated in school rooms, assembly halls, on the campus and in school official

[6] *Ibid.*, pp. 42, 43. *Public Papers of Governor Smith*, Albany, 1920, pp. 277ff.
[7] *New York Times*, May 9, 1921, p. 5.
[8] *Ibid.*, Oct. 7, 1922, p. 3.

publications, as well as from the lips of faculty members and . . .

WHEREAS, Known radicals are not only permitted to address students and advocate sabotage and disloyal acts, but invited to do so by faculty members . . .

Resolved . . . that a joint legislative committee be and is hereby created . . . to make a complete and thorough investigation into the above mentioned abuses. . . .[9]

This resolution, as Mr. Chamberlain observes, converted "the proposed investigation into a prosecution before it had been authorized."

Although the McNaboe investigation was limited in its effectiveness by the chairman's leisurely procedure, the Rapp-Coudert inquiry which followed it and which was based on similar premises "resulted in the dismissal of twenty-four teachers, the resignation of eleven and the failure to reappoint an indeterminate number of others."[1]

It is highly possible that some genuine party members were among the victims of this purge. What damage they had done to the minds of the hardy American boys and girls who attended their classes has never been ascertained. There are those who maintain that even greater dents on the young minds have been made by John Dewey's progressive education and other movements. What is abundantly clear is that these punitive expeditions against the schools produced a climate of fear which affected the majority of the state's teachers for more than a quarter century. This resulted in a paralysis of instruction about communism, a refusal to discuss any of its aspects with students, a total avoidance, in and out of school, of the entire subject, and a generation of American men and women who had grown to maturity in total ignorance of the enemy they were expected to fight. It is hardly to be wondered at that to so large a proportion of the American people, a Communist is someone you don't like.

[9] New York Senate Journal, 159th Sess., 1936, I, 50–53. Given in full in Chamberlain, op. cit., Appendix II, p. 225.
[1] Chamberlain, op. cit., p. 151.

In such a climate, also, teachers must have been faced with embarrassments in elucidating for the young mind the changing values of certain pronouncements as they relate to times and circumstance and in pointing out the consequent danger of any absolute prohibition of free thought and expression.

We may imagine, for example, the dilemma of a teacher of American history who must explain to a class of literal-minded children that the United States came into existence in the early summer of 1776 because a group of gentlemen gathered in Philadelphia openly advocated the overthrow of their government by force and violence, and signed a Declaration to that effect.

4

The combined attacks on liberal education by state investigating committees in New York, California, and Washington, and by the American Legion spread the epidemic of fear among teachers over much of the country. When the Dies committee, the House Un-American Activities Committee, and similar groups in the Senate took up the cry, the more courageous of the educators brought their hostility to the investigations into the open. This hostility whose fire was fanned in the years following World War II by the activities of Senators Jenner, McCarran, and McCarthy burst into sporadic riots in which students supported the teachers. The hottest of these took place in San Francisco while the HUAC was holding its fourth consecutive hearing in that city as late as 1960. It was estimated that some five thousand persons took part in the protests led by students of the University of California. They demanded the abolition of the committee. According to the *New York Post's* correspondent, the police acted with unprecedented brutality toward the protesting pickets, yet of the sixty-four who were arrested only one was held.[2]

The following year (1961) there occurred an incident at the New York State University at Brockport, N.Y., which revealed a conspiracy between the HUAC and the American Legion to interrupt the university's educational program and frighten its

[2] Donner, *op. cit.*, pp. 1ff.

teachers because some of the braver professors had demanded, in a wholly constitutional manner, the abolition of the House Un-American Activities Committee. The leader of the movement, Dr. Edward R. Cain, Associate Professor of Government, tells, in an article in *The Nation*,[3] what happened when they approached their representative in the House, Congressman Harold Ostertag.

The approach was in the form of a petition, signed by thirty members of the faculty, calling for an end to HUAC as a standing committee. Mr. Ostertag sent a polite acknowledgment stating that he was sorry to disagree with the faculty's views. This reply came at the start of the university's spring break, and Dr. Cain left for the vacation concluding that, for the moment at least, there was an end to the affair. But the professor underestimated the vindictiveness of the federal legislative body. To him, the House would either accept or reject the petition; it did not occur to him that this great chamber of the United States legislature would try, like a small boy, to get even.

> While spending the Easter holiday in Boston [he goes on to tell] I received a telephone call from a colleague at Brockport. Congressman Ostertag had sent our faculty petition to the district commander of the American Legion in nearby Rochester. The Legion had photostated copies of faculty signatures and circulated them among local Legionnaires. Telephone calls to the college president had come in from Washington, New York City and Indianapolis, wanting to know what he was doing about the Reds on campus.[4]

The president was alarmed because he thought the Legion might have enough influence in local politics to bring about the defeat of the next state educational bond issue, thereby depriving the university of necessary funds. At the end of the holiday, therefore, he summoned Dr. Cain and asked him to inform Repre-

[3] Edward R. Cain, "The Legion Invades a Campus" in *The Nation*, Sept. 9, 1961, pp. 135*ff.*
[4] *Ibid.*, p. 135.

101

sentative Ostertag and the regional Legion office that the petition did not represent an official faculty petition, "but merely the opinion of certain individual members."

About three days later, the president called me to say that some non-local police officer had asked his secretary for an appointment the following day. He did not know what kind of police was involved, and speculation ranged from a HUAC investigator to the FBI. It turned out to be the New York State Bureau of Criminal Intelligence. Two investigators arrived. One interrogated the president in his office for over two hours and then swore him to secrecy; the other roamed the campus and quizzed students about faculty who had signed the petition. Before they left, the investigators demanded files from the president's office on all thirty signatures. Upon calling state university officials in Albany, the president learned he had to comply with the demand.

Evidently the combined pressure of a Congressman and the American Legion had been effective enough to launch a state police investigation of state university faculty. . . .[5]

No specific charges were brought either by police or the House Committee on Un-American Activities. This was not HUAC's way. Its method was to insinuate guilt by indirection, to call the attention of the community to police investigation and thus to cast suspicion upon wholly innocent men who had been outraged by years of this sort of snake-in-the-grass activity in the Congress of the United States.

It is doubtful that the police states in Europe were based upon such American episodes, although we may at least have supplied the Soviets with some useful hints. It is more likely that the attempts to create a police state in the United States were influenced by a study of the Russian secret police—a study which was denied, of course, to American school and college students.

[5] *Ibid.*

VII. The Atomic Spies

THERE CAN BE NO DOUBT that for many years there has existed, in the United States, an elaborate system of espionage maintained by the Soviet Union. From immemorial time, nations have spied upon one another. In the American Revolution, there seemed to be a British spy under every bed. Some of these were useful to General Washington. When he put on his demonstration of the accuracy of American riflemen on Cambridge Common in August, 1775, he welcomed the attendance of British spies, and it is thought by several historians that the stories they sent home about American marksmanship helped Washington's army win the war.[1] German spies in the late 1930's and early 1940's did much to maintain fifth columns in Czechoslovakia, Norway, the Netherlands, Belgium, and France, and Allied spies, notably British, aided the underground in France, in preparation for the Normandy invasion in 1944, and the partisans in Italy in 1944 and 1945.

It is true that the most conspicuous examples of espionage have been in wartime. Yet a certain amount of it is carried on continuously, often through diplomatic channels, especially if one of the spying nations is suspicious of another or under the threat of war. We know there were Nazi spies in the United States before we entered World War II and, in 1942, several Nazi saboteurs

[1] Roger Burlingame, *March of the Iron Men*, New York: Charles Scribner's Sons, 1938, p. 127. Charles W. Sawyer, *Firearms in American History, 1600–1800*. Boston: published by the author, 1910. John J. Henry, *Campaign against Quebec*, Watertown, N.Y.: Knowlton and Rice, 1844, p. 91.

were captured with their equipment. In running down the saboteurs, who landed at three points along the Atlantic coast, the FBI
did one of the great jobs of its career. This was done, as it should
be, secretly, without an eye on headlines or other publicity.

There are American taxpayers who wish that, instead of spending their money on the will-o'-the-wisp hunt for the long-past
misdeeds of Alger Hiss or the alleged but unsubstantiated pro-
Communist operations of Owen Lattimore, Harry Dexter White,
John Carter Vincent, and many others, the United States Intelligence had used it to spread our own espionage network over the
Soviet Union. The one attempt in this direction which has come
to light was given the most publicity of all when our President
admitted that the function of the U-2 pilot operating in the spring
of 1960 was, indeed, to penetrate Soviet mysteries.

From the establishment of the Dies Committee in the House
of Representatives in 1938 into the critical days of the 1960's,
the Communist espionage conspiracy has steadily increased its
strength. This is admitted by all the anti-Communist agencies.
None of them can or will claim the slightest diminution in the
effectiveness of Soviet espionage in the United States as a result
of their combined efforts. On the contrary, they take pains to
show that its influence has multiplied in the schools, in youth
organizations, in the world of entertainment, in the churches, in
the armed forces, and in the foundations. This admission is, of
course, politic for if these agencies conceded any weakening of
the enemy, their hope of continuation would fade.

In an unintentionally comic leaflet[2] which gives much publicity
to the two front-line fighters against Communist influence on the
arts in America, Congressman George A. Dondero of Michigan
and sculptor Wheeler Williams of New York, Mr. Williams is
quoted as saying at a July, 1959, HUAC hearing, "I would say
that they [the Communists] have been successful beyond their
wildest dreams."[3] This statement implying that the efforts of the

[2] *Minutes of a Communist Cell on Art,* Fullerton, Calif.: Educational
News Service, 1960.
[3] Hearings, House Committee on Un-American Activities, July 1, 1959,
testimony of Wheeler Williams.

Dies Committee, the House Un-American Activities Committee, the Senate investigating committees, the American Legion, and the heroic work of Dondero and Williams have been largely ineffective must have been encouraging indeed to Soviet Intelligence, whose operatives probably take special delight in reading such booklets as this.

Not only this fanatic propaganda, however, is packed with admissions of Soviet success but most of the statements of committees and other self-styled anti-Communist agencies suggest all too constantly that the Russians have been a jump ahead of us all the way. The *National Review*, which calls itself "the nation's leading magazine of hard-hitting anti-Communism and *intelligent* Americanism," in introducing James Burnham's *The Web of Subversion*, joined the chorus.

> You learn the appalling facts [writes William A. Rusher, the publisher] about how materials for *at least* 20 atomic bombs, stolen by subversives, may still be in this country, triggered for use when Moscow gives the signal. You see how the Red network infiltrated key book reviews . . . how easily they duped Liberals like Acheson, Rockefeller, Lippmann, Cousins and Morgenthau. . . . Above all James Burnham shows how Communist infiltration *continues to this day* . . . [Italics in the original.][4]

The book also shows, apparently, "what we can do to wipe out this vicious menace to our possessions, our freedom, our very lives." Yet in the years since this book first instructed Americans how to "wipe out" the threat, Communist espionage has evidently gained headway and strength. In the latest hearings of the HUAC, the charge was reiterated that the Communists have the upper hand. As this charge is an obvious way of scaring the American people into championing the continuance of the committee, it is under suspicion. In any case, would it not increase our confidence in the effectiveness of the fight if HUAC or its

[4] Circular letter of William A. Rusher, publisher of *National Review*, promoting *The Web of Subversion* by James Burnham, New York: John Day Co., 1954.

Senate counterparts could point to a single triumph over the subtle enemy other than the jailing of Alger Hiss for an alleged lie about what he did twelve years before?

In the war against subversion several persons have been tried, convicted and punished (two with death) for telling the Russians secrets about nuclear bombs. There is no evidence to show that the United States or any western power retaliated by obtaining from Russia the information on this subject she must possess to have advanced so far ahead of every other nation in rocket engineering. As Telford Taylor writes in his preface to a revised edition of *Grand Inquest:*

> If it be assumed that traitors in our midst gave the Russians our nuclear bomb secrets, certainly it was neither spies nor traitors who provided the information for Soviet rocket propellants far more powerful than our own. No one has blamed the missile gap, if such there be, on Klaus Fuchs or the Rosenbergs.[5]

As to the laws passed by Congress as a result of investigations, Milton R. Konvitz in his book *Fundamental Liberties of a Free People* has this to say:

> Despite the grave, and even somber, tone of Congress, serious doubts may be expressed as to the effectiveness and wisdom of its enactments in combating Communism. Much of it is like catching rain in a sieve.[6]

It is the opinion of Professor Robert K. Carr, as expressed in his exhaustive inquiry into the peak activities of *The House Committee on Un-American Activities, 1945-1950,* that much of the committee's work has not only not aided but has actually hindered the fight against Communist espionage.

[5] Taylor, *op. cit.,* p. 4.
[6] Milton R. Konvitz, *Fundamental Liberties of a Free People,* Ithaca: Cornell University Press, 1957, p. 337.

It is possible [he writes] that the House Committee put the Department of Justice on its mettle and thereby stimulated it to achieve the successful results that it did in prosecuting espionage agents. But the committee's criticism of the department's enforcement of the espionage laws was at times so partisan and vituperative that it probably succeeded only in antagonizing the department. There is little in the record to reveal that the committee ever successfully performed the traditional role of Congressional investigating committees by revealing shortcomings in the law enforcement program of the executive branch or by helping the latter to overcome these shortcomings. Moreover, at times the committee's own efforts to investigate espionage activity unquestionably hampered the department's simultaneous law enforcement activity in this field.[7]

None of the investigating committees, the societies of professional patriots, or the witch-hunting writers has ever revealed the true and terrible danger of the Communist conspiracy to the American people. This has been disclosed, however, in the clear and simple words of Alan Barth in his *The Loyalty of Free Men:*

Nothing that the agents of communism have done or can do in this country is so dangerous to the United States as what they have induced us, through the Americanists, to do to ourselves.[8]

2

The Sixth Column has not only failed to weaken the communist conspiracy in the United States; it has not only repeatedly drawn herrings across trails that would have led enforcement agents to the true spies and conspirators; it has not only done nothing to encourage counter-espionage *in Russia* where the control of the conspiracy is centered; but it has undermined positive American resistance to the Communist menace.

[7] Carr, *op. cit.,* p. 451.
[8] Alan Barth, *The Loyalty of Free Men,* New York: The Viking Press, 1951, p. 94.

The loyalty programs which it has initiated have kept some of the best men out of government. Talented persons with original ideas which may be controversial have been reluctant to put themselves in a position to be constantly spied upon, to subject their reputations to suspicion and potential ruin. From the very start, a candidate for an important federal post feels that the cards are stacked against him. The moment such a post is offered him, he is assumed by the guardians of loyalty to be guilty and must prove his innocence by answers to a cross-examination which is designed to trap him.

If he is finally "cleared"—a term which implies previous guilt —he soon learns to conform his thoughts and opinions to a norm of mediocrity.

> Federal workers [writes Professor Carr] have learned that it is wise to think no unusual thought, read no unusual books, join no unusual organizations and have no unusual friends. What this has cost the government in terms of loss of independence, courage, initiative, and imagination on the part of its employees is impossible to say, but it is clear that the cost has been great. . . . For this result the House committee [on Un-American Activities] must assume a large measure of responsibility.[9]

While, in the Soviet Union, the recent emphasis had been on education—especially in the pure and applied sciences—the American Sixth Column had spent the taxpayers' money attacking the schools, causing the dismissal of good teachers and preventing the employment of others, attempting to obstruct the lectures of such internationally renowned men as Bertrand Russell and Robert Oppenheimer, and branding some of America's greatest scientists as "disloyal" or "security risks."

Perhaps the most cynical performance in the history of the House Committee on Un-American Activities was its attack on Doctor Edward U. Condon, director of the National Bureau of

9 Carr, *op. cit.*, pp. 456, 457.

Standards. Condon is one of America's most brilliant and learned physicists, an atomic expert, a master of the theory of radio engineering, a profound student of mathematical philosophy, and a member of some of the most important European scientific societies.

The charge against Condon, brought by a so-called "Special Subcommittee on National Security of the Committee on Un-American Activities," was that "from the evidence on hand" the physicist appeared to be "one of the weakest links in our atomic security."[1] The subcommittee making this report was a wholly informal group trumped up by Representative J. Parnell Thomas, then chairman of the House Committee, for publicity purposes. The reason for the subcommittee was that it could act without the knowledge or support of the full committee, some of whose members might object to such outrageous charges.

The way had been carefully paved for this report. The year before (1947) the Washington *Times-Herald* (then a Patterson paper) had been advised that Dr. Condon was about to be investigated, and published two articles to that effect. In the same year, Mr. Thomas wrote articles which were published in nationally circulated magazines attacking Condon. Condon protested, formally, to HUAC, but his protests were ignored and his request for a hearing was not granted.[2]

The report, when it came, was not, therefore, a complete surprise, though even those who had expected it were hardly prepared for so personal and so undocumented a diatribe. It gave a selective biographical sketch of Condon, the items chosen for their innuendo and with snide references to his wife, who was of Czechoslovakian descent, manifestly intended to rouse suspicion as to her "un-American" background.

The report also quoted a letter sent to Secretary of Commerce

[1] *Report to the Full Committee of the Special Subcommittee on National Security of the Committee on Un-American Activities,* Mar. 1, 1948. *New York Times,* Mar. 2, 1948.

[2] Washington *Times-Herald,* July 17, 1947. *American Magazine,* June, 1947. *Liberty,* June 21, 1947. Carr, *op. cit.,* p. 132.

109

Averell Harriman by the FBI in May, 1947, giving derogatory information about Condon taken from the supposedly secret files of the Bureau. It stated the Condon had been

> in contact as late as 1947 with an individual alleged, by a self-confessed Soviet espionage agent, to have engaged in espionage activities with the Russians in Washington, D.C. from 1941 to 1944.[3]

Basing its action upon this irresponsible gossip, the House Committee demanded that Secretary Harriman either remove Condon or come forward with a statement "setting forth the reasons he had been retained." Following this demand by the legislature upon the executive branch of the government, the Department of Commerce announced that in the week before the report of the subcommittee was issued, the department's loyalty board had unanimously held that "no reasonable grounds exist for believing Dr. Condon is disloyal."[4]

Thus, giving to the world its confidential file material, the Federal Bureau of Investigation got in on the act.

If this had been a sincere inquiry by the full House Committee on Un-American Activities, however erroneous, it might be regarded as just another of the committee's mistakes. That it was, on the contrary, a wholly disingenuous money-raising venture, is indicated in this item which appeared in *Time* magazine following the report's release. This was a comment that reflected a wide contemporary opinion.

> New Jersey's Representative J. Parnell Thomas [stated the weekly newsmagazine on March 15, 1948] knows that a good headline come appropriation time, can do more than months of hard work. Last week, as his Committee on Un-American Activities applied for a whopping $200,000 allotment from the House, Thomas dug deep. What he fetched up was an old file

[3] *Report to Full Committee, op. cit. New York Times*, Mar. 2, 1948. Letter to Harriman dated May 15, 1947.
[4] *New York Times*, Mar. 2, 1948.

on Dr. Edward U. Condon, director of the National Bureau of Standards . . .

The *Time* account concluded, after citing the Commerce Department's denial:

But the ineffable Mr. Thomas got what he wanted. The Committee on House Administration approved his request for $200,000.[5]

Condon was more immediately fortunate than many of the other smear-targets of so-called congressional investigations. Instead of losing a job he found one. The heads of Corning Glass Works, aware both of Condon's immense usefulness and the absurd injustice of his persecution, offered him the post of director of its research and development laboratories. This personal compensation to him, however, was only temporary.

In October, 1954, Richard Nixon, then vice-president, and naturally intent on the use of the new broom in Washington, asked for a revocation of the clearance of Dr. Condon pending a new investigation. As a result, Secretary of the Navy Charles S. Thomas "revealed" that there was new evidence sufficient to warrant reconsideration of the Navy's previous security clearance and it was therefore suspended. Condon then said that he had been "fully cleared" four times by four different boards and would be "pleased to be cleared a fifth time."

Two months later, however, when Condon, because the Corning company was about to take on government contracts, was assigned to non-classified work, he withdrew his demand for further clearance and resigned from his position as research and development director for Corning Glass. His reasons for this, according to an announcement by the company, were that his health and efficiency had been impaired by his clearance fight, that he saw no possibility of a fair and independent judgment in his case "at the present time." He had been cleared several times

[5] *Time,* Mar. 15, 1948.

by the military and sensitive government agencies and was "unwilling to continue a potentially indefinite series of reviews and re-reviews."[6]

As a result of the reckless persecution of Condon, wise scientists shied away from government work. This reluctance to cooperate with government was later increased by the judgment in 1954 of two members of a three-man board appointed by the Atomic Energy Commission that J. Robert Oppenheimer, a key figure in the atom bomb project, was, though loyal, a bad security risk, and Senator McCarthy's charges of subversion among scientists at the Army Signal Center at Fort Monmouth.

Referring to the climate of fear that the Sixth Column has induced among scientists, Telford Taylor gives a formula to be followed by one who wishes to be safe.

> To be scientifically reliable today it is prudent to disapprove of "liberal" commentators and desirable to espouse such as Fulton Lewis [Jr.] or George Sokolsky; it is not as safe to belong to the American Veterans' Committee as it is to be a member of the American Legion; above all it is necessary to approve—heartily and enthusiastically—the new attitudes and security standards which are being cultivated and formulated in this atmosphere.
>
> Inevitably, under these circumstances, the security system becomes a device which can be exploited by ambitious, unscrupulous or jealous men, or even by those who simply are in violent disagreement with each other.[7]

Mr. Taylor speaks of Dr. Oppenheimer's exile "under stigma from the atomic world which he had done so much to shape" as "an unforgivable and shameful blunder of which the Kremlin is likely to be the ultimate beneficiary."[8] Dr. Vannevar Bush, who can be relied on as being as familiar as anyone with the labora-

[6] *Facts on File*, vol. XIV, no. 730, Oct. 22–25, 1954, p. 358, and vol. XIV, no. 737, Dec. 10–16, 1954, p. 417.

[7] Taylor, *op. cit.*, p. 300.

[8] *Ibid.*, p. 301.

tory atmosphere, is quoted by the *New York Times* as saying that government scientists "are discouraged and downhearted and feel that they are being pushed out, and they are. . . . They go on working but they feel that they are not welcome; that they are regarded with suspicion . . . and that their security and loyalty are in doubt." Testifying before the House Committee on Government Operations, Dr. James Killian, President of Massachusetts Institute of Technology, said he believed that

the whole problem of security procedures and policies at the present time may be one of the things that is most hazardous to our future research and development activity in this country in relation to military problems.[9]

Again, in the *Time* story on Condon:

For scientists in the Government, already weary of being investigated, checked and rechecked, the Condon case seemed close to the last straw. The staid American Physical Society, of which Condon is a former president, warned that actions like these "will make difficult the collaboration between scientists and the Government on which so much of our future depends. . . ."

Others made a point that the egregious Mr. Thomas had overlooked. His blundering tactics had undoubtedly aided the Communists. The Government's whole loyalty program would be jeopardized if confidential testimony given in a confidential inquiry were subjected to public review at the whim of a congressional committee. As the New York Herald Tribune said: "These blunderers and publicity seekers are approaching a problem which is subtle and delicate as a watch with a monkey wrench and a sledge hammer. The ineffable Mr. Thomas [is] our society's greatest single gift to Communist infiltration."[1]

[9] House Report 2618, 83d Cong., 2d Sess., Aug. 4, 1954, p. 37.
[1] *Time,* Mar. 15, 1948.

3

While these things were going on in the United States something quite different was happening in the Soviet Union. Americans did not know this, for the Sixth Column would not let them be told anything about Russia except that its people were ignorant barbarians controlled by a government that was a gang of villains. Those who, not convinced that such a nation could in less than half a century have become so powerful, inquired further. These "eggheads" or "dangerous intellectuals" discovered that the entire Russian school system had been revamped, that teachers, instead of being held in contempt and paid starvation wages, occupied one of the most esteemed positions in the Soviet hierarchy and were paid salaries relatively comparable to the earnings of American professional ball players or boxers. Furthermore students, during their school and university years, instead of being required to pay tuition were supported by the government. The result was that maturing Russians were probably better instructed in certain directions than any people on earth. The emphasis, to be sure, was heavily on science, pure and applied, and the humanities took second place. Nevertheless these subversive American inquirers behind the Iron Curtain found that, while modern music and painting were officially tampered with, some of the arts such as the ballet and music were as well advanced in Russia as at home.

The eggheads, therefore, were spared the series of rude awakenings during the late 1940's and the 1950's which stunned most of the American people.

The first awakening came in September 1949 when it was disclosed that Russia as well as the United States possessed the atomic bomb. Attempts were made to show that this was because traitors had communicated "the secret" to Soviet spies. The explanation did not satisfy those who had studied the infinitely laborious and complex work that had led to the Los Alamos experiment in 1945. Whatever "secrets" may have been betrayed it was obvious, to anyone who was capable of reasoning, that unless the Soviets had an immense background of research the secrets

114

would have availed them little. They had, moreover, the assistance of captured German scientists to match our Von Braun.

The second awakening came in 1953 when the Soviets exploded their hydrogen bomb, a feat which evidently involved an exploration into an ingredient which could be substituted for one that was in short supply in Russia. The third and hardest shock of all came in 1957 with the news that the Russians had launched the first earth satellite which they called "sputnik"—a triumph which Americans had not yet achieved.

So, the ignorant barbarians had beaten the "greatest scientific nation on earth," the United States, to the draw. This news had an impact on American opinion which caused it to change its tune and take eggheads out of the doghouse.

Perhaps it was this that induced Herbert Philbrick, one of the few American spies on communism who kept his head, to suggest that

> our young people should demand that their schools and colleges provide them with information about communism. This is not being done now. There are very few schools and colleges which have adequate courses concerning communism. This they should demand because it is impossible for them (or for anyone) to fight an enemy unless they know that enemy.[2]

Whether, as Mr. Philbrick spoke thus in February, 1960, to the House Committee on Un-American Activities, there were red faces among his listeners, is not recorded.

It was in that same year of 1960 that HUAC uncovered what it thought was one of the most sensational Communist plots in its history in the demonstration of students against the committee in San Francisco. The picketers, quite peaceful for the most part, were handled with what was probably the bloodiest savagery in the history of police brutality in the United States. They were, according to a reporter who was an eye-witness, "clubbed,

[2] Hearings, House Committee on Un-American Activities, *Communist Training Operations*, part 2, pp. 1324–25, Feb. 2, 3, 1960.

115

beaten, soaked with high pressure fire hoses, and dragged kicking and screaming by white-helmeted policemen."

After the so-called riot was over, HUAC retaliated against the "Communists" who had "inspired" it with one of the most dishonest performances in the annals of even that unscrupulous organization.

Stepping, for the moment, out of its legislative role, the House Committee prepared a motion picture film entitled *Operation Abolition.* By cutting, editing, and "interpreting" the film footage subpoenaed from the news departments of San Francisco television companies they produced a very largely fictitious picture. All scenes of police brutality were cut, and the narration, in a sequence of cynical lies, explained that the violence was all perpetrated by the students—"dupes," the narrator said, of Communist agents.

This "documentary," when completed, was produced in some seven hundred prints and sold to schools or American Legion posts throughout the country. Its distribution was one of the committee's most effective instruments in the spreading of a new fear epidemic.[3]

No one has yet explained, however, why intelligent Communists should strive so hard to abolish a committee which, for some twenty years, has given such aid and comfort to communism.

[3] The *Washington Post,* Nov. 26, 1960. *San Francisco News–Call Bulletin,* Jan. 26, 1961. *The Christian Century,* Jan. 4, 1961, p. 5.

VIII.   Hollywood Sixth Column

CERTAINLY NO ONE in his senses could accuse the House Committee on Un-American Activities of intentionally or consciously giving aid and comfort to communism. Certain members of this committee have sincerely tried to explore the potentials of domestic communism and to expose those American Communists who, they believe, espouse overthrow of government by force and violence as well as others they are convinced collaborate with Communist espionage in the United States. Certain members, however, have always used the committee as a tool for their own political advance and as an instrument of publicity. But neither the sincere nor the cynical members are aware of the subtle devices by which the Communist machine works. They are not aware that the constant and wide publicity given to their anti-Communist efforts is precisely what the real undercover agents of the spy network want; it gives them the opportunity to work quietly beneath the noise and it sends the committee's hounds barking up the wrong trails. How many Communist spies have gone underground as a result of this and other committees' hunts is something only the more penetrating investigators of the FBI can discover—provided they are not hampered by having the door opened on their necessary secrecy by untrained, celebrity-happy, amateur sleuths.

Thus the Communists have been able to scare us out of our free democracy—the only bulwark we have against their invasion. The Federal Bureau of Investigation, though it sometimes violates its own rules and allows congressional committees to intimidate it into unwise disclosures, is nonetheless competent to pursue and catch spies employed by foreign governments: that is what it is for, what it has the machinery and equipment to do, and what it has successfully done in the most urgent of the spy cases. It would be good if the FBI could plug the leaks by which its own information gets out (as in the Condon case) and the cracks in its foundation through which committee members peer and occasionally crawl. Unfortunately its own over-zealous director shares the committee's estimate of the value of publicity.[1]

2

Where the lunatic-fringe anti-Communists, the Legion and the HUAC, have most conspicuously erred is on the Pacific Coast. Here, they have had the help of the California Un-American Activities Committee, an organization more fanatical and misguided, if possible, than the congressional one, and the eager Joint Legislative Fact-Finding Committee on Un-American Activities of the State of Washington. Seattle, Washington, was the scene of early violent demonstrations in which the Legion participated against the I.W.W., and Centralia, Washington, provided the setting for riots instigated by the Legion in the course of which occurred the bloodiest lynching of a white man in American history.

Nothing in the past, however, compared in potential publicity value with the projected investigation of the movie industry in Hollywood in 1947. By that time a large part of the American public had become disillusioned with our brave ally of two years before and were returning to their old custom of looking for Communists under every bed. Always aware of such trends, J. Parnell Thomas saw his opportunity. He had, indeed, so he said, been "besieged with demands and requests" that his committee search beneath the luxurious beds of Hollywood and, in response to this overwhelming clamor, appointed a subcommittee to prepare the way for a full-dress investigation.

[1] 92 CR 5218, 5219.

It was Mr. Thomas's custom to appoint a subcommittee to do the spade-work and, without interference or objection by the more conscientious members of the full committee, secretly to build up a case which would be foolproof when it came to the rigged public hearings. In appointing such a group of advance scouts, Mr. Thomas usually made himself its chairman, and so it was with the subcommittee of three—Thomas, John McDowell and John Wood—which traveled to Los Angeles on May 5, 1947, well fortified by professional staff investigators, "to initiate an extensive and all-inclusive investigation of possible Communist activities and influences in the motion picture industry." All the subcommittee wanted, Mr. Thomas explained to representatives of the press who had come to meet the party, "were the facts." There would be no public hearings. Everything would be done behind closed doors in what were known as "executive" sessions.

These private meetings were a common device for obtaining testimony which a witness might be reluctant to give in public, but which was recorded in order that much of it might be disclosed at a later public hearing. Many a witness has testified in good faith at a secret hearing only to have his trust later betrayed and his confidential testimony published for all to read. Having promised the press that nothing would be known of what happened in the California hearings, Mr. Thomas proceeded to invite a number of "friendly" witnesses to appear before his little group and tell how terrible everything was, naming names and citing chapter and verse of the complex and subtle subversive activities behind the screen.

The witnesses he picked were key men in the industry—directors, producers, screen writers, actors, and actors' managers. Such persons are not noted for their aversion to publicity and one may imagine that they might conceivably have enjoyed the sensational picture they presented. A month later this picture was spread over the *Congressional Record*[2] and though it was not

[2] The complete account of the doings of the subcommittee is given in "Extension of Remarks of J. Parnell Thomas of New Jersey in the House of Representatives, Friday, June 6, 1947," 93 CRA 2687*ff*.

119

precisely stated there who said what, the names of the witnesses were given. The explicit details were reserved for the Washington hearings in November.

In the report to the full committee, published on June 6, 1947, the subcommittee divulged its discovery that "scores of screen writers who are Communists have infiltrated into the various studios and it has been through this medium that most of the Communist propaganda has been injected into the movies"; that some of the most flagrant Communist propaganda films were produced as a result of "White House pressure," that Communist screen writers have employed "subtle techniques" in pictures, "glorifying the Communist system and degrading our own system of Government and institutions"; that "the National Labor Relations Board has given great aid to the Communists in their efforts to infiltrate and control the motion picture industry"— here the committee joined in degrading an American institution —and that Communists have prevented good American pictures glorifying America and the American system from being produced.

In conclusion, the subcommittee recommended to the full committee (Thomas, in short, recommended to Thomas) that it "intensify the investigation with the view of holding a public hearing in Washington before the full committee at the earliest possible date." As a final recommendation, Mr. Thomas, in a not uncommon spasm of partisan feeling, advised Mr. Thomas to "determine the responsibility and extent of the influence and interference on the part of Government agencies or officials in the production of flagrant Communist propaganda films."[3] No glorifying of American government here! Not, at any rate, while Mr. Truman was living on Pennsylvania Avenue.

November, 1947, turned out to be the earliest possible time for the public hearings and with them the House Committee to investigate Un-American Activities started on the most conspicuous fiasco of its career—owing mainly to the incorrigible sense of humor characteristic of American journalists.

[3] *Ibid.*

120

3

Perhaps one reason why the American people as a whole were not immediately responsive to the Hollywood bugbear which the committee went to such pains to expose was that the public at that time was confused about world events. Since 1939, Americans had been forced into a performance of mental acrobatics unprecedented in the history of American opinion. The Hitler-Stalin pact of 1939 which gave the German Nazis the opportunity of starting the second World War without fear of Soviet opposition and which had caused large numbers of American Communists to leave the Party, had spread a wave of hate across the United States—at least in those large areas in which anti-German sentiment was fast increasing. "A plague," said Americans, "o' both your houses"; Nazis and Russian Communists were two of a kind, ganged up against the free world. When the Soviets waged their brutal, aggressive war against Finland, the hatred became more acute. The American Communist Party, despite the pretensions of Martin Dies, was never weaker than in the early spring of 1940.

But then the attention of Americans, with the exception of Dies, his fellow isolationists and a few pro-Germans, was diverted to Hitler's attacks in Scandinavia, Belgium, Holland, and France with their accompanying horrors. For a year, more and more Americans adhered to the Allied cause until a movement began in the United States to "fight for freedom." But it was a bad year on the Allied fronts and by June, 1941, when the Battle of Britain had begun, the entrance of Russia, brought on by the treacherous Nazi attack, forced most of us to forget our anger of the recent past and to welcome the Soviet Union as a partner. Even the most luminous of all anti-Communist statesmen, Winston Churchill, welcomed her.

War does strange things to men's minds and emotions. Everything becomes black or white; the shades of color, the nuances of normal thought disappear, and in all the world there is nothing but good and evil engaged in mortal conflict. Because the Russian people made a truly magnificent defense of their land

121

against the archenemy of mankind, the Russian government must be good because it, too, was fighting the antichrist. It must have reformed. It must have eschewed all its past wickedness, turned over a new leaf, purged itself of its impurities—done all those things that single-minded men put into such platitudes.

To decent folk in their exalted war mood, it was inconceivable that the Communists in Russia were still, under the privations and sufferings of their heroic soldiers, planning the world empire that they called world revolution; that their Comintern which they had expediently dissolved in the hope of more lend-lease would rise again after the cease-fire, more powerful and destructive than ever with a new name, and that the Bear who, for a time, had walked like a man, would walk again like a bear, carrying corruption into a good world.

In this mood, we gave Stalin everything he asked and to do so was perfectly normal behavior. His armies were standing between us and defeat. The American anti-Communists—except, perhaps, the professional ones—kept repeating the cliché: "After all when your house is on fire, you don't inquire into the morals of the firemen." So, when pro-Russian propaganda appeared in the United States it was encouraged. When editorials in the press praised the Russians, no one looked under the editors' beds. When radio commentators spoke favorably of Russian military victories, no one searched the broadcasters' cellars and closets for spies. To root for Russia was the thing to do.

Then, abruptly, in the pattern of mental acrobatics, it was the thing to do no more. When, in the first post-war years, the Soviets repudiated their "reform" and Churchill called attention to the iron curtain that stretched from the Baltic to the Adriatic, the witch hunters had a field day. For now they could point to all the patriotic gestures that had been made toward Russia in the brave flag-waving days as having been the inventions of Communists, fellow-travelers, and radical subversives.

Mr. Thomas was especially exuberant as the Hollywood material of this genre fell into his lap.[4] There were, for example,

[4] Carr, *op. cit.*, pp. 55–79.

four films produced during the heroic days, which became controversial later. There was *Mission to Moscow*, based on the book by former American ambassador Joseph E. Davies and produced by Warner Brothers in 1943; *Song of Russia* produced by Metro-Goldwyn-Mayer in the same year; *North Star* produced by Samuel Goldwyn also in the same year; and *None but the Lonely Heart* produced the following year by RKO. These various producers believed that, in addition to the large receipts they got from the popular films, they had made patriotic gestures useful to the war effort.

In 1947, therefore, after the American public mind had turned its last somersault, the Thomas committee could point to all these pictures as evidence of dangerous Communist infiltration into Hollywood, a movement which had made "dupes" of all the screen writers, directors, actors, and technicians and induced them to betray their country and the "American Way" by participating in the productions.

Best of all, however, these movies provided Thomas and his Republican and southern Democrat colleagues with powerful political ammunition against the New Deal. Obviously the pictures had not only been inspired in the White House but they had been produced, moreover, under White House pressure. Thomas's sub-committee even gave out the news that Robert Taylor had admitted in executive session that he had been forced to postpone his enlistment in the navy in order that he might act in *Song of Russia*—an allegation that he later emphatically denied in public hearing.

If I ever gave the impression [said he] in anything that appeared previously that I was forced into making *Song of Russia*, I would like to say in my own defense . . . I was not forced because nobody can force you to make any picture.[5]

The "friendly" witness against *Song of Russia* was Ayn Rand,

[5] *Hearings regarding the Communist Infiltration of the Motion Picture Industry*, p. 167.

123

the writer who, in several subsequent books has taken a position
so far to the extreme Right that she has been subjected to much
ridicule by the literary critics. Of her appearance before the subcommittee, Professor Carr writes:

> Miss Rand then proceeded to give a 4,000-word detailed
> scene-by-scene analysis of *Song of Russia* that could only have
> been the product of a mind obsessed with a fear and hatred of
> all things radical. Even such conservative members of the
> committee as John Wood and John McDowell were obviously a
> bit skeptical about her vehement attack upon the film.[6]

Those who know Miss Rand and know of her personal background in her native Russia are aware that her strong feeling
against everything Russian was almost inevitable; it is interesting
therefore, to find that Mr. Thomas picked her as one of his star
witnesses.

In a forthright manner, Louis B. Mayer, head of the MGM
studio, explained precisely the conditions under which *Song of
Russia* was made.

> Mention has been made of the picture *Song of Russia*, as being
> friendly to Russia at the time it was made. Of course it was. It
> was made to be friendly. . . . It was in April of 1942 that the
> story for *Song of Russia* came to our attention. It seemed a
> good medium of entertainment and at the same time offered an
> opportunity for a pat on the back for our then ally, Russia. It
> also offered an opportunity to use the music of Tschaikovsky.[7]

Of the Warner Brothers production, producer Jack Warner
said in public hearing:

> If making *Mission to Moscow* in 1942 was a subversive activity,
> then the American Liberty ships which carried food and guns

[6] Carr, *op. cit.*, p. 64.
[7] *Hearings . . . Motion Picture Industry*, p. 71. Carr, *op. cit.*, p. 63.

to Russian allies and the American naval vessels which con-
voyed them were likewise engaged in subversive activities.
The picture was made only to help a desperate war effort and
not for posterity.[8]

Despite this statement, Mr. Warner was badgered and persecuted by the committee's adroitly savage staff investigator but
at last replied repetitively to the investigator's repetitive questions:

We were in the war and when you are in a fight you don't ask
who the fellow is who is helping you.[9]

Similar defenses were made by the producers of *North Star*,
"the first major attempt," stated the review in *Time*, November 8,
1943, "by a major U. S. producer [Sam Goldwyn]"

to present Russia's war with the Nazis in the way that Winston
Churchill saw it when the war began—not primarily as a
struggle for Communism, but as a heroic defense by the Russian people of their homes. Only by implication is *North Star*
revolutionary propaganda.
It is the first attempt to draw the vast struggle into some
graspable unity by typifying all Russia's resistance to the Nazis
in the resistance of one Russian village.

The attack on *None but the Lonely Heart* demonstrates the
confusion in the minds of the committee and its staff about what
is subversion. To them it was apparently subversive to present
poverty on the screen. To them the very existence of poverty
anywhere in the world implies the presence there of Communists.
None but the Lonely Heart was not about Russia but about
London's East End. It was called by *Time's* severe cinema critic
"a feather in the cap of all concerned in its making." "In the

[8] *Hearings . . . Motion Picture Industry*, p. 10.
[9] *Ibid.*, pp. 38–39. Carr, *op. cit.*, pp. 61, 62.

125

U.S.," he continued, "major productions have rarely dared to tackle so wholeheartedly so harshly human a subject."[1] But one factor in this non-Communist film which gave the committee a handle was its writer-director, Clifford Odets, who had participated in other proletarian shows. Yet the *Time* review makes the point that Odets had "subdued" his sociology and used "ideological restraint."

Contrasted with this implication that poverty and communism are bedfellows is the Thomas subcommittee's statement that the Screen Writer's Guild is

> under the complete domination of the Communist Party. These writers receive anywhere from $500 to $5,000 per week.

4

After the first Washington hearings in November, 1947, the history of the Hollywood investigations by HUAC is shrouded in mystery. Suddenly the hearings stopped. Thomas insisted that they would soon resume and for some time continued to insist that this would happen any day, yet they did not resume until four years later in 1951. By this time Thomas had resigned in disgrace from the Congress following his conviction on criminal charges in connection with alleged "kickbacks" from the salaries of his office staff, and served his time in the federal penitentiary at Danbury, Connecticut.

One explanation of the adjournment was that the committee's chairman had been disappointed in the response of the press. It was not that the journals and magazines had attacked the committee; far worse, they had ridiculed it. *Time,* for example, burlesqued the hearings from start to finish. It depicted Thomas's "bald plate glistening in the hot glare of the Klieg lights,"[2] "his red neck swelling" and his gavel smashed in anger.[3]

---

[1] *Time,* Nov. 20, 1944, p. 92.
[2] *Time,* Nov. 3, 1947, p. 22.
[3] *Ibid.,* Nov. 10, 1947.

Right on cue, [stated *Time,* referring to friendly witness Adolphe Menjou] a dapper, greying man in a brown double-breasted pin stripe, wearing a pair of heavy shell-rimmed glasses sauntered jauntily up to the witness stand. As the applause quickened, he turned, bowing and smiling to his expectant audience, maneuvering his profile skilfully in the fusillade of exploding flash bulbs. With forefinger dramatically outstretched, he raised his hand for the oath.[4]

A point in Menjou's testimony which the writer of the *Time* story emphasized was the actor's "surefire if somewhat simplified method of spotting" Communists:

Anyone attending any meeting at which Paul Robeson appears, and applauds, can be considered a Communist.[5]

Rupert Hughes who later took the stand, "too had a simple way of identifying Reds: 'You can't help smelling them.'"
Concluding its story, *Time* commented:

The real trouble with the Thomas committee seemed to be the committee itself. Instead of buckling down to the problem of Communism where it hurt, as in the labor unions, it had gleefully pounced on Hollywood, where the publicity was brightest. It had failed to establish that any crime had been committed—*i.e.,* that any subversive propaganda had ever reached the screen.[6]

Again, then, HUAC, led by its headline-hunting chairman, had barked up the wrong trail while the real spies and infiltrators had exulted in this diversion. Though it has not been specifically recorded, American Communists must have been sadly disappointed when the hearings ceased.

[4] *Ibid.,* Nov. 3, 1947.
[5] *Ibid.*
[6] *Ibid.,* Nov. 10, 1947, p. 26.

127

Unluckily for them, the press had almost unanimously condemned the investigation of the motion-picture industry. Its instrument of ridicule, the one weapon the humorless Thomas could not stand, had defeated him.

The *New York Herald Tribune* commented on October 22:

Some attempt was made to show that Communism was being permitted to creep into films, but in each case the attempt dissolved into the ludicrous. . . .[7]

And, after the committee had abandoned the investigation, the *Herald Tribune* remarked

This may be taken—perhaps ungraciously—as Mr. Thomas's confession that the Hollywood investigation has been producing a good deal of nonsense and nothing else.[8]

5

Of course there have been Communists in Hollywood; there probably still are. There are Communists everywhere. There are all sorts of Communists in America; some are crackpots and harmless; others are theoretical Communists, persons who believe that goods and enterprises should be owned in common by all members of a community but who have no intention of enforcing their beliefs in town, state, or nation. There are spies and espionage agents and saboteurs, trying to induce Americans to join them, usually with marked unsuccess. Herbert Philbrick discovered these people by pretending he too was a Communist but even he, with all his talent and observation, could not discover any really significant triumph by the conspirators.

There are Americans who would do anything for money; others who would do anything for power. Yet there are few Americans who would exchange the America they have for a state watched

[7] Oct. 22, 1947. Carr, *op. cit.*, p. 75.
[8] Nov. 1, 1947.

over, restricted, and controlled by a Big Brother who pries into every incident of their private lives. Many a man will betray his country for personal gain but few would care to continue to live in the country they have successfully betrayed. Many will use the freedom American citizenship or residence may give them to aid and comfort a powerful enemy but they would not care to live without that freedom in a land they have helped the enemy to take over.

There is little sense in the wish so often expressed by "friendly" witnesses that all the Communists go "back" to Russia—forgetting, for the moment, that a large proportion of such persons are of the third American generation. But the real wish is to get rid of these people, to get them out of the way rather than to stand up to them here. This is a symptom of cowardice, a concession of fear, rather than a patriotic stand on an American tradition, one which says: "I am an American; show me something better before you can persuade me to change my allegiance."

The aim of Communists, who are working for the so-called world revolution, is to make other nations so much like themselves that the transition to totalitarianism will be almost imperceptible. This is happening in the United States. Under the delusion that we are fighting them we are adopting, one by one, their own tactics; piece by piece, their own strategy. We have already, in certain instances, allowed them to dissolve many of the safeguards of our peculiar form of democracy: the separation of powers, the rights of the individual to due process, and the preservation of the private dignity and freedom of judgment that our Constitution has given to every citizen.

These things the Communists are trying to do to us. They know that panic is the ideal culture for the germ of communism. That is why we should hate, not fear, them. Profiting by the colossal blunders made by our legislatures, they have undermined us in ways so subtle that the masses of Americans, following like sheep abstractions such as "subversion" or "un-Americanism," cannot grasp nor gauge them.

Yet it is not too late. Let us forget all our cloak-and-dagger melodrama. There is only one word to answer; a word all Russians understand. The word is No.

"Nyet."

IX. Presumption of Disloyalty

In APRIL, 1945, Franklin Roosevelt died and Harry Truman automatically became president of the United States. In the following summer, the second World War ended and its end, accompanied by the shock of the sudden entrance of the atomic age, left Americans in the kind of postwar confusion that has become a recognized historical necessity. Though its confusion was not so profound as that which followed the Civil War nor so spectacular as in the aftermath of the first World War, yet it was aggravated by new elements and by factors unique in history.

The war had not been a war to end war by the will of mankind as romanticists had declared in 1919; yet it appeared to be the war to end war by technological development. The conviction that some substitute for war would have to be found if life on earth was to continue was confronted with the condition of irreconcilable political patterns and ideologies which promised to grow further apart. And the public mind was exhausted by the sequence of mental acrobatics which, as we have seen, had been forced upon it since 1939.

In August, 1945, the curtain had come down; yet the dancing in the streets had scarcely stopped before perceptive Americans knew that the curtain would soon rise again upon a new and tragic act. By March, 1946, it had risen. The narrator, standing under the proscenium as it rose, was Winston Churchill. In words that may never be forgotten, he warned of the scenes to come as he told of the line "From Stettin in the Baltic to Trieste in the Adriatic" that had come to divide the continent of Europe.

131

Behind that line lie all the capitals of the ancient states of central and eastern Europe, Warsaw, Berlin, Prague, Vienna, Budapest, Belgrade, Bucharest, and Sofia, all these famous cities and the populations around them lie in what I might call the Soviet sphere, and all are subject, in one form or another, not only to Soviet influence but to a very high and in some cases increasing measure of control from Moscow. . . .

Except in the British Commonwealth and in the United States, where communism is in its infancy, the Communist parties or fifth columns constitute a growing peril to Christian civilization. These are sombre facts for anyone to have to recite on the morrow of a victory gained by so much splendid comradeship in arms and in the cause of freedom and democracy, but we should be most unwise not to face them squarely while time remains. . . .[1]

Listening to, or reading this speech, fear-prone Americans discounted Churchill's exceptions of the British Commonwealth and the United States. In Canada, indeed, a spy-ring had just been exposed. No, this speech—since famous because, among other things, it introduced the phrase the "iron curtain" into our language—alarmed, and was intended to alarm, us. From the American point of view, it was the opening gun of the cold war.

To many, it gave the not uncomfortable assurance of settling back, after all the Nazi and Japanese threats and attacks, into the prewar mood of anti-communism. This seemed a natural, normal mood for Americans; after all, the Russians were the first villains and the people behind the Axis were clean decent people led astray by psychopathic war lords.

And, as Churchill said, we must face the "sombre facts" squarely; now was the time; now before it was too late; and from this impetuosity came the extremes which, early in the 1950's, began to undermine the foundations of the Republic.

There have been, especially in postwar confusions and dissillusionments, a considerable number of Americans who, giving

[1] Speech delivered at Westminster College, Fulton, Missouri, Mar. 4, 1946.

lip-service to democracy, have secretly envied the totalitarian systems. They have been impatient of the delays that democracy imposes. They have yearned for decrees, backed by force; they have felt that a strong and preferably secret police, acting on reflex rather than reflection, could sweep our society clean over-night of spies, traitors and foreign agents. They have ignored or discounted the fact that along with this highly kinetic action go concentration camps, mistaken identity, firing squads without benefit of jury trial, the midnight knock at the door, the arbitrary arrest, the *incommunicado* confinement, the stifling of speech, and the control of thought.

A Federal Bureau of Investigation was not, to these totalitarian thinkers, enough. In spite of the FBI's performance—excellent, of course, as far as it was allowed to go—congressional investigating committees, on the "infallible" testimony of ex-Communists, were discovering the heavy infiltration of the executive departments of the government by disloyal and subversive Americans. If we were to face the "sombre facts" as Churchill advised, we must strengthen the whole security apparatus. We must cut short the delays imposed by the obsolete tradition of "due process"—we must, in briefer words, become totalitarian ourselves in order to meet a totalitarian menace.

2

In January, 1947, Harry Truman, President, though not spe-cifically elected to that office by the people, found himself in the not unprecedented position of a Democrat with a Republican congress barking at his heels. The Republican senators and representatives elected in November, 1946, were not only hostile to Truman's administration; their enmity was retroactive. Their target was the New Deal and all its works; the New Deal was their scapegoat; it had brought them to this pass. Exactly what "this pass" was, in 1946, will probably not be clear to later historians. The United States had just emerged unconditionally victorious from the most formidable war on record; it had suf-fered little material damage at home while much of Europe was in ruins; it had developed the atomic bomb and held it uniquely, and it was at a pinnacle of power in a war-exhausted world: the cynosure of foreign eyes and again, as Turgot said in the days of its new independence, the hope of mankind. At this point, the committees dedicated to the exposure of subversion were pleased to lead the Congress into a new panic.

President Truman was fully aware of the inevitable consequence. He knew that the committees, motivated now by political antagonism as an increment to their zeal, would soon find, or pretend to find, a host of "security risks" in every executive corner, would blame his administration for their presence and would continue to blame it for the employment, in the future, of such characters. He therefore anticipated this action by creating, by executive order, a new Loyalty Program to be applied to all incumbent employees in the executive departments and all applicants for jobs there. There can be little doubt that he did this reluctantly; and whether, in the light of ethical theory, he should have done it at all is debatable. But as a politician, he saw no alternative.

Executive Order 9835 provided that each department, bureau and agency should have its own loyalty board from whose decisions appeal might be made to a Loyalty Review Board. The Review Board was to provide a hearing for any employee or applicant charged with disloyalty by a Regional Board. At this hearing, he was allowed to appear with counsel and to present witnesses and affidavits.

The program was thus presumably hedged with a device for giving "protection," in the words of the order, "from unfounded accusations of disloyalty." This sounded reasonable and in accord with the requirements of the Bill of Rights regarding "due process." The President, however, was counting, so to speak, without his host. His host, in this instance was the Federal Bureau of Investigation.

Other provisions of the executive order permitted the FBI to throw a monkey wrench into the machinery which would render the entire Loyalty Program impotent to administer justice. One

134

such provision was that every investigation should begin by a name check against the files of the FBI, the Civil Service Commission, and the military and naval intelligence services. If any "derogatory information" was thus disclosed, there might be further checks against the files of the House Committee on Un-American Activities, files of local government agencies at the suspect's place of residence and school and college records. Even if the FBI played no part in the loyalty probe, "due process" procedure might be interrupted; but it was certain to be stopped cold at the start by the check against the FBI files.

It is an essential regulation of the FBI (though, as we have noted, not invariably observed) that the files of that police agency be kept confidential. The reasons for this are obvious. No detective operation can be successfully pursued unless its leads are veiled in secrecy. It will appear in a trial that Criminal A has been informed upon by Witness B but the police investigator cannot give out this information until A has been apprehended.

Thus, while the FBI may unearth so-called "derogatory information" about a government employee or applicant for a government job, it is unable to give the source of that information or produce the informer to be cross-examined as to his credibility, character, or motive—a procedure guaranteed to a defendant in any court of law. The Loyalty Review Board, therefore, denied its accused the privilege expressly provided by the Constitution of the United States of confronting the witnesses against him.

The FBI's information may have come from irresponsible gossip, from persons motivated by jealousy or vengeance, or from congenital liars. It is the bureau's rule, however, that it may not evaluate the material in its files. Thus true and false testimony, authentic and hearsay evidence, documented facts, and malicious gossip are all lumped together without distinction. That, at least, is the theory. There have been cases in which spokesmen for the bureau have admitted screening its witnesses. While the rule holds, however, leaks from the files which are given publicity and

135

so are subject to reckless evaluation by the public may be exceedingly dangerous.

The injustice of the Loyalty Board's performance soon came to light in a number of cases investigated by the boards.

In 1948, James Kutcher was removed from his position as clerk in the Veterans Administration and was declared "disloyal to the United States." As a test of loyalty, the absence of both his legs, lost in the Battle of San Pietro in 1943, was regarded as inferior to his membership in the Socialist Workers Party—an organization which, in spite of its firm denial of intent to alter the government by violence, has been declared subversive by an attorney general.

> The Attorney General's ruling [writes Alan Barth] makes him [Kutcher] therefore the victim of a dual arbitrariness. The organization to which he belongs has been arbitrarily held to advocate what it denies advocating. And this advocacy was imputed to Mr. Kutcher through the mere fact of his membership—an assumption of guilt by association which the Supreme Court in the Schneiderman case denounced as invalid and repugnant to American law. This arbitrariness, moreover, has cost Kutcher much more than his job; it has cost him a reputation for loyalty to his country earned at considerable sacrifice in its military service.[2]

A more celebrated case was that of Dorothy Bailey, who had worked for a government agency for fourteen years and had been promoted at intervals. During that time her salary had increased to more than five times her original pay. Her educational background included graduation from the University of Minnesota and graduate work at Bryn Mawr College. She had been so trusted a worker that, although she was dismissed in June, 1947, because of a reduction in force, she was rehired less than a year later. Upon being rehired, she was, technically, an applicant and so had to pass her regional loyalty board.

[2] Alan Barth, *The Loyalty of Free Men*, New York: The Viking Press, 1951, p. 108.

This board dug up a rumor to the effect that Miss Bailey had been "a member of the Communist Party or the Communist Political Party" and had "attended meetings of the Communist Party." She also, according to the report, had "associated on numerous occasion with known Communist Party members." She denied these allegations and answered others with statements that obviously refuted any disloyalty implication. Nevertheless she was refused her re-employment—and took her case to the Loyalty Review Board.

There her counsel stated that the allegations were "a result of malicious, reckless gossip which has no foundation in fact," asked repeatedly for the names of the informants and was refused with the statement by the chairman of the board that they were judged reliable by the FBI. Apparently, in this case, the Bureau had not enforced its wise rule against evaluating the material in its files. The accused then testified in her own behalf, repeating her denials, and presented some seventy supporting affidavits. But neither she nor her attorney was ever told who the "stool pigeons" had been.

When the United States Court of Appeals sustained the judgment of the Loyalty Board, it stated that "it has long been established that if the Government, in the exercise of a governmental power, injures any individual, that individual has no redress." As in many cases, however, a dissenting opinion seemed more valid than that of the court. Rebutting a popular contention that government has a right to hire and fire whom it pleases without giving reasons therefor, Judge Henry W. Edgerton maintained the government had no right to inflict severe and permanent punishment of individuals in its service without recourse to a court of law.

Dissenting, Judge Edgerton contended that "dismissal for disloyalty is a punishment and requires all the safeguards of a judicial trial." Dismissal for incompetence or for some other reason . . . or for no reason at all, is not punishment; but dismissal for wrong conduct or for wrong views is punishment;

137

for a "person dismissed as disloyal can obtain no normal employment, public or private." Miss Bailey was, therefore, entitled to all the safeguards of a judicial trial, including trial by jury, clear information of the charges against her, and confrontation of accusing witnesses.[3]

It is possible that if the investigations of the loyalty boards were secret, the punishment might be mitigated. But these inquiries, unlike those taken by a private or non-governmental employer, are given full publicity; the official black mark becomes as conspicuous as Hester Prynne's scarlet letter. Thus, a discrimination is made between governmental and private employment which is extremely weakening to government services. Whereas a private employer may not accuse an employee of crime or felony without being called upon to have his charges proved in court, the government may call its workers disloyal —and while disloyalty by itself is not, technically, a crime, it is publicly regarded as such—with no responsibility whatever to sustain its charge.

The end result is that government service today is dominated, on most levels, by a cult of mediocrity. One has only to visit any of the lesser offices of, say, the State Department to find oneself in the midst of timid persons largely inarticulate because of the requirements of conformity. They are afraid to express any opinion lest it appear to be unorthodox. This condition is largely the result of the Loyalty Program, of which Mr. Barth says:

It is a program that tends to eliminate or silence individuality. It tends, too, to undermine the morale of federal workers by making their tenure uncertain, by making them distrustful of their colleagues and by making them subject to constant anxiety. At a time when the government imperatively needs the best talent procurable, this is a serious risk to national security.[4]

[3] Konvitz, *op. cit.*, p. 264.

[4] Barth, *op. cit.*, p. 128. On the effect of loyalty investigation on civil servants, Morton Grodzins, *The Loyal and the Disloyal*, Chicago: University of Chicago Press, 1956, chap. 13.

As we review the progress of loyalty testing—or, rather, disloyalty testing—we get an image of the infiltration into this supposedly free country of Soviet practice that is more alarming than all the plots, real or imagined, to overthrow our government by force and violence. No espionage that has ever been discovered is as subversive as the distortion of our constitutional patterns and the traditions of our way of life which has come with our panic decision to "fight fire with fire." If we can combat communism only by adopting its methods, then the fortifying concepts of liberty and human rights on which our society has relied for some two centuries are not as strong as the Founding Fathers supposed them to be.

3

In what James Wechsler has called the "age of suspicion" it has become customary to demand of persons applying for certain positions a "loyalty oath." In most state, county, and municipal positions, this usually follows a fine-tooth combing of the sort described in federal practice. In the oath, the applicant swears that he has not done and does not intend to do any of the things about which the researches have been made. Thus the oath becomes, not strictly a loyalty oath, but rather a non-disloyalty oath.

The official word for the investigation is "clearing." Until the applicant is "cleared" he is unacceptable. Cleared of what? one may ask. Cleared of any guilt which probably lies in his past. In other words, he is presumed to be guilty until he proves himself innocent—a reversal of the presumption under which Anglo-Saxon judicial processes operate. He then swears that he is not, never has been and never will be a member of the Communist Party or any organizations on the Attorney General's subversive list, after which the magistrate says to him in effect, "Go and sin no more."

Some sort of oath of office has usually been required of those about to occupy public posts. These, however, have until recently been positive oaths. Also they have applied to the future only, not the past. One expects to promise to support and defend

139

the Constitution of the United States and of the State if it be a state job; to defend the community against its enemies, domestic and foreign, and to carry out the purposes of the office to the best of one's ability. But only in the age of suspicion has the negative entered the wording of the sworn statement: that one is *not* and *never* has been a member of the Communist Party, that one is *not* affiliated with subversive organizations, that one does *not* sympathize with those who advocate overthrow . . . and so on. Refinements of this oath express denials not only of acts but of thoughts: it must lay open the rooms of the mind which our constitutions and common law have given us the right to keep locked; it must invade, in short, the privacy which is one of the guarantees of our way of life.

In the age of suspicion, moreover, this invasion is no longer confined to government workers; it has been directed into one of the most sacred provinces of our domain, that of education. For reasons that are far from clear, teachers have become, after government employees, most suspect of subversion or at least of "radical" and "left-wing" tendencies. The only explanation of this is that any independent and inquiring mind—the presumed property of an educator—must explore unorthodox as well as conformist thought. Having discovered such things as the philosophy of Marx or the thoughts of a Bertrand Russell, a John Maynard Keynes, a J. Robert Oppenheimer, or a Julian Huxley, it is assumed that he will not only tell his pupils about these things but do all in his power to induce the students to espouse them. This will at once force the impressionable young mind into radical, socialist, or atheist molds. In our schools, then, will develop the generations of vipers who will eventually overthrow the government of the United States by force and violence.

As one would expect, teachers have been the most articulate rebels against the loyalty oath requirement. Yet many a man and woman have lost and are continuing to lose important jobs because of refusal to swear away their mental freedom. And many more who, having taken the oath, are accused of violating it because some gum-shoe principal or supervisor has overheard snatches of a lecture on Communist theory or because some irresponsible boy or girl, courting favor, has misquoted a professor of philosophy or economics. The alleged offense may have occurred in the classroom but it may also have taken place far from the school, in private conversation with a pupil in his home or elsewhere or, indeed, to a colleague or complete outsider in a club or at a private dinner. For example, a New York State commissioner of education issued a memorandum designed to implement the regulations on subversion which stated:

> Nor need such [subversive] activity be confined to the classroom. Treasonable or subversive acts or statements outside the school are as much a basis for dismissal as are similar activities in school or in the presence of school children.

In 1958, Congress passed a bill the main purpose of which was applauded by senators and representatives alike. It provided for loans for needy students seeking college education. It contained one paragraph, however, which for many eager students vitiated the entire act. This required that those applying for the loan sign an affidavit declaring that they do not believe in or support any organization which believes in or teaches the overthrow of the government by illegal methods.

Although many students who were headed for the nation's leading university or schools of higher education might willingly have signed the affidavit, Harvard, Yale, Mills, Grinnell, Sarah Lawrence, and many other colleges and universities and several of the best science laboratories said No. They would not accept students who had been forced through lack of funds to sign the affidavit. They believed that this provision in the act caused a violation of academic freedom, and though considerable hardship was caused by their stance, they refused to participate in a program so circumscribed.

In connection with the subsequent debate in Congress on the question of loyalty oaths in education it was resolved to reprint in full in the *Congressional Record* an article published in

141

Coronet in April, 1960, entitled "College Loyalty Oaths," by Senator (later President) John F. Kennedy.

The Senator began his piece by quoting Benjamin Franklin who had regarded oaths as "the last resource of liars." Nevertheless, Kennedy went on:

> In times of crisis to the state—times of war, insurrection or suspected subversion—both Federal and State Governments have repeatedly sought some swift, convenient and reassuring means of publicly identifying and compelling citizen loyalty. Elaborate loyalty oaths and affidavits—going far beyond the simple pledge of allegiance or the oath to uphold and defend the Constitution—have inevitably been the answer.
>
> But there is no evidence that they have ever contributed substantially to the security of the Nation.

Senator Kennedy then reviewed the recent events that had led to the oath epidemic.

> Between the end of World War II and the end of the Korean war, a rising tide of fear and suspicion engulfed many Americans. The detection of Communist agents and the erection of new standards of loyalty and security were no longer left to responsible authorities. Neighbors, fellow workers, faculty members, Federal employees, friends—anyone might turn out to be "Red" (or said to be by someone). Easy answers and convenient scapegoats were sought and provided, in a troubled time when the answers—How did the Russians get the bomb? Why did we lose China?—were not easy.
>
> But one easy answer was the oath. Those who took it were loyal; those who refused were not. What could be simpler? And so countless hundreds of new oaths sprang up, administered by Federal, State and local bodies: oaths for school teachers, oaths for notary publics, oaths for professors, students and scientists and, in one State, a loyalty oath for professional wrestlers.

Then, looking with questioning and dubious eyes toward the future, Kennedy continued:

Surely this is not the way to "catch up" with the new Russian excellence in education, science and research—by imitating their objective of teaching students what to think instead of how to think. What kind of security is it that assumes all is well because thousands of affidavits are signed: do we really believe that loyalty can be reduced to an automatic formula, coerced and compelled instead of inspired?[5]

Thomas Jefferson, writing to prospective members of the faculty of the University of Virginia, gave what is perhaps the best definition ever formulated of academic freedom.

This institution will be based on the illimitable freedom of the human mind. For here we are not afraid to follow truth wherever it may lead, nor to tolerate error so long as reason is left free to combat it.

Perhaps if these words were inscribed over every gate to every American campus it would free our young people from fear of the whole truth—a fear that haunts the Kremlin and that will eventually defeat Russian communism.

[5] Reprinted 106 CR 8663 (Apr. 25, 1960).

X. Security and Liberty

THE HISTORY of the Federal Bureau of Investigation brings into the same focus two divergent directions of American thought which the Bureau, in its maturity, has resolved. One tends toward a distaste for formal police; the other insists on the conviction that each American is his brother's keeper. In the nation's adolescence, the end result of this dichotomy was the formation of vigilantes, community groups that took trial and punishment into their own hands. The logical conclusion of the vigilante impulse was the Ku Klux Klan, but we may see vestigial indications in those sallies of the Sixth Column that by-pass what the Constitution calls "due process."

In the opening years of the twentieth century, a decade or two after the geographical frontiers had closed and the "conquest" of the continent was thought to be complete, formal police operated in most communities and judicial trials replaced the drumhead variety. Even cattle "rustlers" in the sparsely settled West were brought into court. Both courts and police, however, were local institutions. Except in Texas where the Rangers were graduating from vigilante status, the image of state police was repugnant and the concept of a federal police force was associated in the common mind with foreign dictatorship.

In 1907 and 1908, in the administration of Theodore Roosevelt, this popular view was reflected in the Congress. There, the President's opponents were already protesting his so-called dictatorial methods. When the attorney general introduced the first suggestion of a federal police, horror spread even among the

President's supporters. The fact that the head of the Department of Justice was Charles Jerome Bonaparte, grand-nephew of the Emperor Napoleon, was not conducive to the acceptance of his suggestion. Though the Emperor had refused to recognize his brother's American marriage and exiled his sister-in-law to her native land where the offspring had become bona fide American citizens, a congressional suspicion remained.

In 1907, therefore, the Congress refused to consider the Attorney General's proposal. He persisted, however, in his efforts to get his police force established in the orthodox way with Congressional approval. His arguments seem to us today to be reasonable. In the investigation of violations of the Federal statutes, he was obliged, he said, to borrow detectives from the small forces employed by other departments for strictly departmental protection. The Treasury needed such police to guard the mint. So, too, did the Post Office for the protection of the mails. Why then should not the Department of Justice, whose business it was to promote Federal law enforcement, have its own police to watch for transgressions against interstate commerce laws, for fraud against the government, for violators of admiralty or maritime legislation and other matters which are the concern of federal courts? But this argument so angered the members of Congress that they passed a law forbidding the Attorney General to borrow the policemen of other departments for any purpose whatsoever.

The act precipitated the crisis out of which emerged the FBI's predecessor. Bonaparte waited till Congress had adjourned. Then, on July 1, 1908, he quietly established his agency, calling it the Bureau of Investigation of the Department of Justice.[1] Thus, somewhat in the manner of a vigilante, he took the matter into his own hands without legislative blessing.

When Congress reconvened, hell broke loose, especially in the House.[2]

[1] Annual Report, Attorney-General, 1909, pp. 8–10.
[2] 43 CR 655*ff.* (Jan. 8, 1909).

145

The only question here before the House [said the Honorable George E. Waldo of New York] is whether we believe in a central secret-service bureau, such as there is in Russia today . . .[3] I believe that it would be a great blow to freedom and to free institutions if there should be in this country any such great central secret-service bureau as there is in Russia. We do not need it here in this country, and there ought not to be any such bureau.[4]

Representative Walter I. Smith of Iowa insisted that

no general system of spying upon and espionage of the people, such as has prevailed in Russia, in France under the Empire, and at one time in Ireland, should be allowed to grow up.[5]

2

Between 1908 and 1924, the American scene changed more rapidly than in any equal span in American history. Technology stepped up the tempo to a degree not even today fully grasped by the human, let alone the social, mind. The old, sharply defined state barriers were all but erased by new transportation and communications. This had a centralizing effect, bringing about a new focus on Federal government. The notion that crime was exclusively a local concern was no longer valid in a nation of incessant interstate activity. The escape of an offender across a state line was now so easy that some substitute for cumbersome extradition proceedings seemed necessary.

A highly sensational attempt by Congress to plug a loophole by which a criminal might flee from justice came with the so-called Mann Act of 1910. This followed much open publicity that had been given to commercialized vice. Between 1900 and 1910, studies by various committees and commissions revealed a shocking nation-wide prevalence of organized prostitution. An

[3] Note that this was eight years before the Bolshevik Revolution, while Russia was still ruled by the Czars.
[4] 43 CR 3132 (Feb. 29, 1909).
[5] *Ibid.*, 672 (Jan. 8, 1909).

article in *McClure's* magazine by George K. Turner exposed conditions in Chicago, where ten thousand prostitutes were commercially exploited by combinations of hotels, dance halls, saloons, and disorderly houses. Groups such as the Committee of Fourteen in New York made surveys in other cities and there followed an exposure of what was called the "white slave trade." This apparently national organization operated by luring young girls from rural districts with promises of economic opportunities, with the result that the disorderly resorts were kept well stocked. An inquiry in Pittsburgh in 1907 found two hundred houses of prostitution in one section alone and this was followed by investigations in Minneapolis, Hartford, and Portland, Oregon, and such groups as the American Society of Sanitary and Moral Prophylaxis gave attention to the national picture.[6]

Well, said morally outraged senators and representatives, was not the White Slave Trade, then, engaged in interstate commerce? And was its abolition not, therefore, the business of the federal government? Representative James Robert Mann, Republican, of Illinois and an expert on interstate commerce, thought it was. The bill he introduced provided for the arrest of males inducing females to cross state lines for immoral purposes with the intent of pecuniary gain. It became law in June, 1910, and was known forever afterward as the Mann Act,[7] a designation that gave rise to ribald puns in smoking cars.

Obviously, the implementing agency for this statute was the new federal police force. Such an assignment meant large expansion of the bureau and the elevation of its status. As Max Lowenthal, critical biographer of the FBI, recalls:

The enforcement of the Mann Act began the transformation of the Justice Department's police bureau from a modest agency concerned with odds and ends of Federal law enforce-

[6] Harold Underwood Faulkner, *The Quest for Social Justice, 1898–1914*, New York: The Macmillan Co., 1931, pp. 160–63.

[7] 36 U.S. Statutes, chap. 295, p.825. For debate on the Mann Act, see 45 CR 804-823; 1030-1041.

ment to a nationally recognized institution, with agents in every State and every large city.[8]

Though in the first dragnet operations mistakes occurred and the bureau's detectives soon ceased to discriminate between commercialized vice and personal delinquency, the work of Federal police in protecting pure and innocent young virgins from exposure to sin received wide acclaim and the news that now Uncle Sam had become his brother's keeper made the bureau exceedingly popular. The general public, especially its middle-aged female constituents, took a special delight in seeing young men caught in the private sowing of their wild oats, and punished. Moreover, in the enforcement of the Mann Act, there was an invasion of privacy on an unprecedented scale, for nearly every man who was observed traveling on a train with a woman at his side was suspect and subject to interrogation. And all this, repugnant as it might be to those who still held the views of the Founding Fathers about the rights of the individual, was appropriate to the prevailing moral temper.

3

In general the popularity of the Department of Justice's police force continued until it was reorganized as the Federal Bureau of Investigation in 1924, after which it achieved a heroic status. Its public favor had, to be sure, its ups and downs. During the participation of the United States in the first World War its arbitrary arrests of suspected draft dodgers were widely criticized[9] but were forgiven as inevitable wartime abuses. Less excusable by thoughtful Americans were the postwar raids under the aegis of Attorney General Mitchell Palmer, though in its frightened mood the general public supported extreme measures.

When, however, it was renovated and, in a sense, rebuilt, in

[8] Max Lowenthal, *The Federal Bureau of Investigation*, New York: William Sloane Associates, Inc., 1950, p. 14.
[9] *New York World*, Sept. 5, 1918.

1924, upon a foundation laid by Attorney General (later Chief Justice) Harlan Stone, even the thoughtful critics ceased their attacks and the FBI became an integral part of the American scene. In this year, and the succeeding ten, the bureau was kept busier than ever fighting the organized crime that National Prohibition had stimulated.

Its new director, John Edgar Hoover, soon became a national hero. As the Number One detective, he appealed to addicts of crime mystery stories, and he made the most of that appeal. Though most of his agency's work must be carried on in secrecy, he advertised it as much as was consistent with security. Boys of all conditions became his ardent fans, and it is safe to say that he deterred many of them from criminal careers. The press, eager for releases of dramatic "true stories" by the bureau's informal public relations department, gave them the widest publicity. Even the Director himself gave to the world, in magazine articles and books, vivid accounts of the stalking and capture of criminals of every sort.

Why, then, in later years, was there such bitter criticism of the FBI by such careful and thorough students as Senator Norris of Nebraska, journalist Alan Barth, Max Lowenthal, the late historian Bernard DeVoto, and many others who felt that it had played a part in the subversion of traditional American ideals?[1]

Looking back, we may see a sequence of errors which have hurt the FBI's prestige. Its first mistake was in inviting the cooperation of the public. As soon as it encouraged informers, it began an accumulation of gossip, rumors, malicious accusations, and irresponsible charges which became embedded in its celebrated "files." Although it disclaimed evaluation of this dossier material and ruled that it should be kept strictly confidential, it was inevitable that there should be leaks. Also, when challenged,

---

[1] Norris speeches 86 CR 5664 *et seq.* Barth, *The Loyalty of Free Men,* chap. 7. Lowenthal, *op. cit., passim.* Bernard DeVoto, *The Easy Chair,* Boston: Houghton Mifflin Co., 1955, pp. 169–76.

employees of the bureau were sure to maintain that it had screened the informers.

Second, the bureau was diverted from its original purpose of investigating criminals by the spy hunts in which it co-operated with Congressional investigating committees, to inquire, not into criminal acts but into subversive beliefs. In the initial instances of this, Congress, not the FBI, was at fault. In time, however, the FBI seemed only too glad to give its information to any committee that was engaged in an exposure of espionage. Third, it allowed itself to be drawn into a close liaison with the American Legion and other societies of super-patriots. Finally, the Director angrily resented even the most legitimate criticism of himself and of his bureau and repeatedly implied that such criticism was Communist-inspired.

4

The co-operation of the public began during the bureau's operations in enforcement of the Mann Act. Letters by the thousands poured in accusing Tom, Dick, and Harry of transporting innocent girls into the urban purlieus of sin.[2] Experiments in amateur sleuthing have always been popular among Americans: here was a golden opportunity. Furthermore, unsubstantiated accusations could be used as a means of getting even with a personal enemy. This started the bureau's dossiers. These were greatly expanded when war came and informers told of spies and "disloyal" citizens. From the reorganization on, the assembly of dossiers was a part of the FBI's regular business.

The fifteen years to the outbreak of the war in Europe in 1939 were the heyday of the FBI's career. It was in these years that the bureau built its reputation for efficiency in tracking down kidnappers, bank robbers who escaped local capture, the hijackers, and other gang men who multiplied in the prohibition era. There was little criticism in all this time and the FBI became the object of the almost universal adulation, which, although later it

[2] Lowenthal, *op. cit.*, p. 20.

disturbed Senator Norris, was reflected in both chambers of Congress.

The first change in the bureau's function of detecting criminals and investigating violations of federal statutes came immediately after the start of World War II in Europe, when President Franklin Roosevelt, on September 6, 1939, instructed the Attorney General to instruct the FBI to "take charge of investigative work in matters relating to espionage, counterespionage, subversive activities, and violations of the neutrality laws." From then on, the bureau's professional detectives co-operated with the amateur detectives in the Congressional investigating committees and subcommittees; and in the years that followed, there was increasing relaxation of the rules against leaks and evaluations. Much of this was inevitable. Some of the disclosures of material in the bureau's files were necessary and even desirable in the interest of justice as, for example, in the Judith Coplon case, which we are about to examine. But the fringe damage in this and other cases, due to the indiscriminate filing of facts, rumors, and gossip, was very great. Here the rule against evaluation— often extremely useful in the earlier criminal work of the bureau —turned out to be a cause of character assassination of innocent individuals.

It must be remembered, however, that in all this activity, the FBI was never a conscious part of the Sixth Column. It was merely a tool—often an unwilling or reluctant one—of the Sixth Column which operated in Congress, in the loyalty boards or in private organizations. Unhappily, it was used by the Sixth Column not in detecting criminal acts or in the pursuit of their perpetrators, but in the investigation of beliefs and associations —investigations which invaded the freedom of the mind. Most of this occurred after the close of the second World War when the Russian bear started to walk again.

In 1947, when the postwar Communist spy plot, to the great satisfaction of Sixth Columnists, again reared its ugly head, there occurred an event which was the natural fruit of a natural phenomenon. This was the turnover of FBI personnel. By 1947

151

the bureau had many alumni. In that year a group of these established a corporation called American Business Consultants, whose purpose was to warn employers against persons suspected of fellow-traveling or otherwise subversive thoughts and associations. It first issued a newsletter named *Counterattack,* a publication which could be prepared only by men familiar with the FBI files. Leaks which occurred through this medium were hard to spot, as they were usually presented in the form of innuendo, suggesting that named persons were being watched by the FBI without revealing the specific accusations in the dossiers. This corporation has, according to Professor Carr, "done much to encourage the growth of a vigilante spirit in the United States."

The publishers of *Counterattack* issued, in 1950, a little book called *Red Channels,* in which were listed the names of persons in show business with a notation accompanying each name of the number of times it had been cited by the FBI or an Un-American Activities committee. As no accusation was made, the resulting character assassination was done by innuendo. The most celebrated case of this was that of the actress Jean Muir, who was removed from a television program as a result of the mere inclusion of her name in the list. It was, of course, the authority of the FBI that carried the greatest weight with employers of show "talent."

In 1948, as we have noted, a subcommittee whose chairman was J. Parnell Thomas exploited a confidential letter written by J. Edgar Hoover to Commerce Secretary Averell Harriman disclosing part of an FBI loyalty report on Edward U. Condon. As a result of the hearings, Condon lost his job with the Bureau of Standards.

In this same year, the FBI was used by the Loyalty Boards in President Truman's Loyalty Program with extremely damaging results to individuals. This whole story, including an analysis of the conspicuous cases of James Kutcher and Dorothy Bailey, has been told in the chapter on "Presumption of Disloyalty." So, too, in its place, will be described the use of FBI files by Attorney General Herbert Brownell in his posthumous attack on Harry Dexter White.

152

The most massive contribution of the FBI files to a criminal trial was made in 1948 and 1949 when Judith Coplon, an employee of the Department of Justice, was charged with attempting to transmit classified information to a Russian agent.

Here we may see the FBI facing a dilemma which has resulted from a combination of two of its wisest rules—that protecting the secrecy of its files and that against the evaluation of file material. Miss Coplon's defense attorney demanded that the FBI turn over its entire file on her case, and Judge Albert Reeves sustained him. In this the judge was widely supported by the press. Indeed it is difficult to see how he could have done otherwise. It would have been highly unjust—and indeed unconstitutional—not to have laid before the court and the jury all the evidence against the defendant so that the defense attorney, by cross-examination, could question its competence and validity. On the other hand, the file material, being unevaluated, contained items of gossip, hearsay, stories told by unidentified and unscreened informants, and rumors which concerned others than the defendant—rumors which might injure innocent people.

The first reaction by Mr. Hoover was against allowing the use of confidential documents in the trial. Some critics believe that embarrassment over the revelation of the sort of material the FBI had been collecting had more weight with Mr. Hoover than the reluctance to violate a rule of long standing. In any case, the final decision was up to Attorney General Tom Clark, Hoover's boss. But if Clark supported Hoover in a refusal to turn over the files, he would have to drop the case entirely, a move which would arouse the ire of spy-hunters everywhere.

That [said an editorial in the *Washington Star*] was when Mr. Clark had to make his final decision. He was naturally aware of the embarrassment to the Government—especially to the work of the FBI—which revelation of these voluminous documents, filled with gossip, hearsay, and innuendo against innocent citizens would entail.[3]

[3] June 15, 1949.

153

Clark decided to release the material—all of it. He could not very well eliminate any of it without being accused of "evaluation." So precisely what the *Star* had expected came to pass. The bits the informants had passed to the bureau drew many persons who had committed no offense into the arguments in the court, and wide publicity was given to many irrelevant items.

> There just doesn't seem to be any sense [wrote John Griffin in the *Boston Sunday Post*] to much of the publicity as unjustified accusations are flying around. The result of the disclosure of names . . . is to place a stigma on prominent people without any evidence to justify the charge.
>
> The absurdity was most marked in the case of President Daniel L. Marsh of Boston University, whose name was among the FBI records as possibly a fellow traveler. As far as anyone can judge, his name was sent in to the FBI and recorded without investigation.
>
> If the FBI accepts and makes a record of every name that is being given by anyone, then nobody in the United States is protected against abuse. What is there to prevent a person sending the name of someone he doesn't like into the FBI as a possible Communist?
>
> If the information is accepted and a record is made, it might come out at some subsequent trial, and no matter what sort of denials are made, it will be almost impossible to clear the name.
>
> This is just plain hysteria . . .[4]

On June 9, 1949, the *Washington Post* gave excerpts from an FBI report introduced into the trial. One stated that a "confidential informant" had advised the Bureau that Fredric March, Canada Lee, Daniel L. Marsh, president of Boston University, Clyde R. Miller, a Columbia professor, and Norman Corwin of CBS were "outstanding Communist Party fellow travelers." Another "informant" submitted a list of speakers at a meeting in New York, December 8, 1945, called "Crisis Coming, Atom Bomb

_____
[4] June 12, 1949.

—for Peace or War." The list included Harlow Shapley, Julian Huxley, Senator Charles W. Tobey, R. J. Thomas, Col. Evans Carlson, Dr. Harold C. Urey, Helen Keller, Danny Kaye, Sculptor Jo Davidson, Fredric March, and Henry Wallace. Because shadows had been cast on some of these persons "guilt by association" suggested that all were under a cloud. Another informant saw Helen Hayes act in a skit performed in December, 1945, at a meeting of the American Society for Russian Relief. A fourth informant reported that the name of Florence March was "mentioned" in a conversation between two alleged members of the Communist Party in 1946—a disclosure which subjected the FBI to the accusation of illegal wire tapping. The whole of this revelation shows how, in the trial of one suspect, shadows may be cast on many others, some of them wholly innocent, once the files of the FBI are opened to the public.

The jury and the court were further entertained by a report that an unidentified informant had expressed the opinion that he was "satisfied" that a number of Hollywood actors or writers were card-carrying Communists. The report further tried to fix guilt by association on Fredric March and his wife Florence, persons who had previously been accused by *Counterattack* against which they had brought a suit for a million dollars, a case which was settled out of court and which brought an apology from *Counterattack*. Incidentally one of the reports indicated new unsubstantiated "evidence" of guilt by association of Mrs. Edward Condon.[5]

5

Most of the FBI's critics insist on the Director's personal integrity as well as on his remarkable capacity for handling the most difficult and stubborn criminal cases. Nevertheless, one might wish that there were less showmanship connected with Hoover's office or that the Director would appear less frequently and theatrically before the public in person, through the radio, the newspapers, and signed magazine articles which read like the

[5] *New York Times,* June 12, 1949.

most sensational mystery stories. It in no way impugns Mr. Hoover's honesty to wish, in short, to see him show more of the quiet dignity and the discreet silence one associates with Scotland Yard of London.

But such comment on "dignity" was answered by Mr. Hoover himself (who nearly always answers his critics)—an answer given to someone who had criticized his usual high-flown rhetoric as lacking in dignity.

If it's undignified, [he said without mellowing his language] then I'll be undignified. I'm going to tell the truth about the rats. I'm going to tell the truth about the miserable politicians who protect them and the slimy, silly or sob-sister convict lovers who let them out on sentimental or illy-advised [sic] paroles. If the people don't like it they can get me fired. But I'm going to say it.[6]

This is the sort of "straight-from-the-shoulder" talk that has won him so much popularity, especially among young people. Youth, indeed, is a favorite sounding-board for Mr. Hoover's most picturesque discourses. To graduating classes in universities he has made some of his most celebrated addresses:

The confirmed criminal [he said in a broadcast to the senior class of Drake University] has nothing but sneers for the Almighty. It is the same with the multi-named "fronts" of the foreign "isms" which seek to mire us in the abysmal depths of despair. They should be reviled for what they are, a cowardly, slithering mass of humanity, too evil and too slinking to assume their true identities, crawling to their objectives while concealed in a jungle of deception . . .[7]

Could anything be better calculated to bring shivers to young spines?

[6] Quoted by Courtney Ryley Cooper in his Foreword (p. xviii) to *Persons in Hiding* by J. Edgar Hoover, Boston: Little, Brown & Co., 1938.
[7] Reprinted in 86 CRA 3588.

There is a sneer behind their every smile and a vicious lie in their every promise of Utopia. If the land whose banners they carry is Utopia, then let them go there and enjoy it. America is good enough for us and we do not want it tainted by the poisons of foreign "isms."[8]

In the same year, in another mood, he said to the American Legion (advice not always successful with that patriotic body):

I look to the American Legion to overcome any wave of hysteria that may sweep the country.[9]

His perennial confidence in the Legion was never dented by any of the tendencies we have noted. In the same speech (in September, 1940, following the fall of France) he said:

The American Legion is an important bulwark of our national security. Today your organization takes on an added significance in a period of emergency. . . . Fortunately the Nation can depend on you. . . .
This Nation will be everlastingly indebted to you Legionnaires for your devotion to the principles of our democratic Government . . . the Federal Bureau of Investigation is proud of its close co-operation with your organization . . .[1]

Earlier that critical year, he said to the Daughters of the American Revolution:

. . . I hope today that you will pledge yourselves with me to a solemn rededication of citizenship. That you will give more of your efforts, more of your being, and of your hearts to teaching and emulating Americanism. That you will strive ceaselessly to focus the spotlight of truth upon the "ism" scum which seeks to undermine the foundations of our nation. By doing so you

[8] *Ibid.*
[9] 86 CRA 5896.
[1] Speech to 22d Annual Convention of the American Legion, Sept. 25, 1940. Reprinted 86 CRA 5896.

will illuminate the world with the brilliance of American democracy and demonstrate the sacred character of honest, decent, human elements which, God willing, our Stars and Stripes may forever symbolize.[2]

The spectacle of the DAR illuminating the world is arresting indeed.

There is variety in Mr. Hoover's literary contributions. His book *Persons in Hiding* is a collection of true detective stories with many didactic interludes addressed to boys and their mothers.[3] It is good of its kind and interesting though its effectiveness is not reflected in the statistics on juvenile delinquency. But his *Masters of Deceit*,[4] though occasionally decorated by flowery language, is an extremely careful analysis of communism with more attention to the Marxist-Leninist philosophy and its progress in Russia than to the plots of the American Communist Party.

6

One of the great handicaps to the FBI, according to the late George William Norris who spoke much about the organization on the floor of the Senate, was the almost universal hero-worship accorded it and its Director; a condition not unassisted by the releases from its unofficial public relations staff.

Unless we do something [said the Senator from Nebraska] to stop this furor of adulation and praise as being omnipotent, we shall have an organization—the organization of the FBI— which instead of protecting our people from the evil acts of criminals will itself in the end direct the Government by tyrannical force, as the history of the world shows has always been the case when secret police and secret detectives have been snooping around the houses of honest men. In my judgment unless this procedure is stopped, the time will soon arrive

[2] Apr. 18, 1940.
[3] *Op. cit.*
[4] New York: Henry Holt & Co., 1958.

when there will be a spy behind every stump and a detective in every closet in the land.

The Senator praised some of the "wonderful work" the bureau had done in the past.

But we cannot have it dominated by any individuals or by any groups who are looking to newspaper advertising for adulation every day of their lives, who arrest men and try them in the newspapers and not in the courts of law. . . .[5]

Finally, thought Norris, it was a pity that Hoover's supporters should think criticism of his bureau was a "smear" usually Communist inspired. He told of a well-known columnist who

devoted a whole column to my attempt to smear Hoover.[6]

This caused Senator Henry F. Ashurst of Arizona, a strong supporter of the FBI and its Director, to say:

Charging the able Senior Senator from Nebraska with attempting to smear somebody is about like charging Abe Lincoln with a similar endeavor.[7]

Mr. Hoover himself, however, was not above such accusation of his critics, though he never mentioned Norris by name.

I charge [he told the New York Federation of Women's Clubs] that the most vicious "smear" campaign which is being directed against the F.B.I., is a part of the working program of various anti-American forces . . .
The Communists hope that with the F.B.I. shackled, they can proceed without interference as they go their boring, undermining way to overthrow our Government.[8]

[5] 86 CR 5664.
[6] *Ibid.*
[7] 86 CRA 2794.
[8] Address to Federation at Hotel Astor, New York City, May 3, 1940.

159

Replying to a critical article in the *Yale Law Journal,* a paper surely entitled to take the bureau to task, Mr. Hoover wrote

I find such opinions most frequently expressed on the pages of the *Daily Worker,* the publication of the Communist Party.[9]

Of this, Joseph L. Rauh, Jr., chairman of the National Executive Committee of Americans for Democratic Action, said to the National Civil Liberties Clearing House,

The obvious implication is that anybody who criticizes the FBI is a Communist or a fellow traveler . . . It is true that the Communists and their fellow-travelers do criticize Mr. Hoover. But honest and sincere criticism is needed and deserves a hearing on merits, not motives.[1]

But this sort of imputation is, of course, a familiar Sixth Column tactic and Mr. Hoover, more than most people, should repudiate it. If such vindictive retorts are avoided, if less is done to cultivate the already almost pathological adoration of the bureau than in the past, the truly great achievements for which it deserves all credit will, in the future, not be obscured by behavior which, to say the least of it, is not wholly adult.

[9] Hoover "Comment" in *Yale Law Journal,* February, 1949, p. 410.
[1] Washington, Feb. 24, 1950.

XI. "Ordeal by Slander"

IT IS AS FASHIONABLE in 1962 to hold the late Senator Joe McCarthy in contempt as it was, ten years back, to proclaim that, much as one disliked his methods, he would prove, in the long run, to have been good for the country. This was, of course, another way of saying that the end justifies the means. In times of real or imagined emergency this is a popular view, to be discarded when the emergency either disappears or shifts its focus.

There was, however, a hard core of supporters of the McCarthy brand of extremism which went underground during the reaction from the lunatic interval and now has arisen in a yet more extreme form clothed in a mantle of "rightism" or "conservatism" which it is no longer conventional to call "fascism." This we shall soon consider. But meanwhile, in order that the new movement may be seen in its true colors, it should be useful to review portions of the so-called McCarthyism of the early 1950's, much of which was forgotten in the wave of revulsion which followed the Senator's collapse. It should be useful to review this, not only as a base of understanding of the dangerous current move of the extreme Right toward totalitarianism, but because the wreckage which followed the McCarthy holocaust still lies all about us.

It is undoubtedly true, as Richard Rovere,[1] McCarthy's most critical biographer, believes, that the Senator himself did not act from any deep-seated conviction; that, rather, the beginning of his campaign was motivated by personal political ambition; that his

[1] Richard H. Rovere, *Senator Joe McCarthy*, New York: Harcourt, Brace and Company, 1959, *passim*.

161

discovery of communism was recent and accidental, and that he was surprised at the immediate public response. But it is also true that the time was precisely ripe for his performance. There had been long psychological preparation for public acceptance of his "crusade." Indeed, if McCarthy had not existed it would have been necessary to invent him. These things are evident to any reader of the history of the decade from 1945 to 1955.

Professor Robert Carr, who naturally focuses his attention upon the committees in the House, writes:

> It may be fairly asserted that McCarthyism would never have been possible had not the Un-American Activities Committee and its predecessor, the Dies Committee, paved the way from 1938 on. It may be granted that the Un-American Activities Committee, even in its most irresponsible moments during the 80th Congress, never quite descended to the indecent level on which Senator McCarthy has operated. Moreover, Senator McCarthy began his obscene attacks at a moment when the House committee was trying hard to mend its ways. But this perverse turn of affairs may well prove that having earlier indulged in an irresponsible course of action the committee could not suddenly mend its ways without having someone else seize the initiative from it.[2]

It is, therefore, more important to a study of the Sixth Column to show the building of the platform which McCarthy, in 1950, found ready-made for his electioneering than to examine in detail the psychopathic behavior of the Senator. It is instructive, also, to recall his intimidation of the Senate, of members of certain executive departments and agencies, and of a presidential candidate to a point at which foreign observers talked seriously of a McCarthy dictatorship. Such a review will show McCarthy as a symptom rather than the cause of the panic disease which weakened the nation at a time when it most needed strength.

[2] Carr, *op. cit.*, pp. 455–56.

162

2

In 1947, after the Russians had turned out to be the real villains after all, rather than the Nazis against whom we had fought for four years, and after Churchill's Iron Curtain speech had warned us of Communist fifth columns in other nations (though not in our own), Congressional investigators found it desirable to raise again the specter of a plot to overthrow the government of the United States by force and violence. Since the war, the press had been woefully inattentive to this revival of the old menace. In the case of the motion picture scandal, for instance, it had declined to take as seriously as the committee wished the dire revelations from Hollywood made by J. Parnell Thomas's Un-American Activities group in the House. Furthermore the hearings on this investigation had been suddenly and mysteriously dropped; this fact and the publicity given to Mr. Thomas's personal embarrassments had, by 1948, somewhat reduced the prestige of the House committee. Of this, Telford Taylor writes:

> The Committee held more hearings than before, but its great days were over. In a manner of speaking the Un-American Activities Committee fell victim to its own success in hitting the headlines. Such a powerful engine of publicity and political pressure could no longer remain the exclusive property of one House committee.
>
> For the Senate was about to reassert itself as the investigating chamber *par excellence*.[3]

In the next few years, then, the investigating committees of the Senate committed excesses which went far beyond the most macabre dreams of any of the House chairmen including even Representatives Dies and Thomas. The Senate did not use the word Un-American for any of its groups; rather it adopted the communistic tactic of hiding them behind innocent-sounding "fronts" such as the "Investigating Subcommittee of the Committee on Expenditures in the Executive Departments"—nomen-

[3] Telford Taylor, *op. cit.*, p. 97.

clature which suggested mere watchdog activities meant to curb executive extravagance. Under such a name, however, a committee could do anything it wanted, and this, from 1947 on, the Investigating Subcommittee proceeded to do. Unfortunately, its wish seemed to be to assassinate the characters of persons whose political views differed from its own. In the process, it scrapped for the time being the Bill of Rights.

In the years 1947-1953, the so-called investigations were carried on by subcommittees with various names, chairmen, and memberships. The objectives appeared to be the same. Investigation for the sake of finding a basis for new legislation was not always one of them. Like the anti-Roosevelt Dies and Thomas committees of the House, these of the Senate conducted a series of punitive expeditions against persons supposedly in the camp of the Truman administration, with his State Department the principal target. Curiously bypassing logic, they called as their main witnesses renegades from the Communist Party. While stoutly maintaining that Communists were congenital liars and basically corrupt, they put implicit faith in every statement made by persons who, for years, had been trained in the arts of falsehood and misleading innuendo. But these characters, they said, had at last seen the light and were therefore more reliable than men and women who had consistently remained of sound mind and had been far too intelligent ever to join the Party.

There are, of course, exceptional cases of Americans who, in immaturity or under severe emotional strain, have momentarily embraced communism. This is not necessarily a proof of mental instability. But an American who for long periods of time has acted as an employee of a foreign government in the performance of espionage against the United States does not seem to be a logical candidate for a position of trust in Washington. He may be wholly sincere in his abandonment of subversion and his repudiation of communism; it is the soundness of his mind that remains in question. Does his reform mean that he has wholly overcome the weakness that once led him astray? There are, today, hundreds, perhaps thousands, of former "fellow travelers" who have become equally psychopathic in the anti-Communist

Right; who have jumped, in short, from one lunatic fringe to another.

The first Senate subcommittee in 1947 saw fit, nevertheless, to call avowed former spies as their key witnesses. In a court, defense counsel would have an opportunity to question the competence of such testimony, but the United States Senate does not allow its victims to be represented by counsel and anyone who casts doubt on the reliability of a witness is "unfriendly" and may be declared guilty of contempt.

The witnesses on whom the subcommittee most relied were Elizabeth Bentley and Louis Budenz, both called because of their previous records of disloyalty to the United States. Miss Bentley had already given some lurid testimony before the House Committee on Un-American Activities, another reason for the Senate committee's wish to get her in on its act. Before the House Committee, she had testified as to her soundness of mind and calmness of judgment when, in answer to the question why she had become a Communist, she replied as follows:

> Thinking back on it, is rather hard to remember my state of mind at that particular moment . . . I was quite infuriated with what I had learned about fascism in Italy, and the only people who would listen to me were the people in the American League Against War and Fascism, and, as I said, I gradually got into that, and gradually there I met Communists . . . and gradually my ideas began to change. I suppose, in a way, I was a very confused liberal, and, unfortunately, we confused liberals have a tendency to look for guidance some place and a tendency to admire efficient people who know where they are going and seem to be doing a good job in the right direction.[4]

One of the Communists she met in this search for guidance was one Jacob Golos with whom she fell ardently in love[5] and whose constant association with her over several years failed to

---

[4] Hearings before House Committee on Un-American Activities regarding Communist Espionage, 81st Cong. 2d Sess., pp. 539–40. Cited by Carr, *op. cit.*, p. 90n.

[5] Carr, *op. cit.*, p. 91.

clear her mind. It was not, indeed, until after Golos's death that she came to her senses. Meanwhile, she said, she handed him much classified information which she alleged she obtained from the employees of various government agencies.

"And who were these?" the House Committee had eagerly asked. Her list ranged far and wide from incumbents of war bureaus to the Treasury and, indeed, the White House itself. These included Nathan Silvermaster, Victor Perlo, William L. Ullmann, William W. Remington, Duncan C. Lee, Harry Dexter White, Assistant Secretary of the Treasury, and Lauchlin Currie, a White House secretary. When the Senate subcommittee took Miss Bentley over it focused mainly on Remington.

The "spy-queen," as she was called, testified that Remington while in the War Production Board had met her under the rose and given her classified military information. She said he was or had been a member of the Communist Party. As a result of this testimony he lost the job in the Department of Commerce which he held in 1948. Remington got himself completely cleared by the Loyalty Review Board and was reinstated. Congressional committees, however, are always reluctant to let their victims go, and two years later, early in the period of the McCarthy hysteria, Remington was haled before a grand jury because two ex-Communist informers told the House Committee that he had been a member of the Party when he was eighteen. When he denied this he was indicted for perjury.

The other key witness in the hearings of the Senate subcommittee was a very different type from Elizabeth Bentley. Louis Budenz, professor in a Catholic university, had also been a Communist but he was an intellectual. He was what conformists like to call a "brain-truster" or "egghead"—the sort that for that very reason is often distrusted by politicians, witchhunters, and policemen. Because of his Communist background, however, all else was forgotten and all he said was taken as gospel by the senatorial persecutors.

As managing editor of the *Daily Worker*, Budenz had apparently become a co-conspirator with Elizabeth Bentley and he was

166

able to give added weight to her accusations. He did, however, pick more plausible targets, such as Gerhart Eisler, alleged representative of the Communist International in the United States, and was thought by both Senate and House committees to be a substantial and highly informative informer. Of him, Professor Carr writes:

> His testimony had the ring of sincerity and accuracy, and it unquestionably dealt with a highly significant aspect of the Communist movement. But his presentation was long-winded and disorderly, and the [House] committee showed itself largely unable to direct his testimony on to topics that should have been of great interest to a Congressional body anxious to acquaint itself concerning all phases of Communist activity.[6]

However, Budenz's main usefulness seems to have been in exposing the Party's apparatus and techniques rather than in putting his finger on dangerous individuals.

All of the work by the Senate committee that was trying to take over the glory of its counterpart in the House in the late years of the 1940's was preliminary to, and training for, its really spectacular performance under Senators McCarran, Jenner, and McCarthy. Among their victims were Owen Lattimore, a distinguished scholar, teacher, and expert on the Far East; and the man who was, perhaps, the greatest American general since Grant and Lee, George Catlett Marshall.

3

Before passing judgment on these committees' pursuit and persecution of individuals, we should review a phase of American history which may not be completely interpreted for another half-century.

Russia's entry into the war against Japan preceded by only a few weeks the end of that war. This was long enough, however, for the professional anti-Communists in America to build a case

[6] *Ibid.*, p. 291.

against all those Americans, from President Truman down, who had agreed to Russian participation. It is true that the Soviets reaped advantages from that short participation out of all proportion to the effort they exerted toward victory and that these greatly increased the power and encouraged the imperialistic ambitions of the Soviet Union. But this is hardly sufficient reason to apply the brand of treason to men who sincerely tried to bring order out of chaos in China and hoped to establish harmony between revolutionists and nationalists there. Yet this is precisely what certain powerful members of Congress did for some five years, inflicting wounds which may never heal and spreading lasting fears and suspicions among the American people.

These men and their supporters became known as the "China Lobby." Their thesis was that the United States was responsible for the defeat of Chiang Kai-shek's forces and the consequent victory of the Chinese Communists. It is improbable that any of them actually wished to send American armies to reinforce the Nationalists but they believed, apparently, that the Generalissimo could have licked his enemies if only we had not betrayed him into Communist hands. The extremists held that the State Department, arm of an administration of which they disapproved, had engineered the betrayal, using as its agents Owen Lattimore, John Carter Vincent, General Marshall, and others. The facts in the case, such as that Lattimore was not an employee of the State Department and was not even its adviser, did not bother the China Lobby or Senator McCarthy who had, indeed, never concerned himself with facts. All that was necessary was to assert that Lattimore was a tool of the Department, because the Senator knew that once this label was attached to him it would be hard to unstick it.

Lattimore's statement when the attacks on him began makes clear not merely his accusers' disregard of facts but their contempt for them.

I knew [he later wrote] why I had already been sniped at by the China Lobby. It was because I had enough firsthand knowledge to form independent judgments. I was not a captive of the Chiang Kai-shek line, the China lobby line, the State Department line, or the Old China Hand line. The China Lobby wanted a simplified propaganda picture of China with all-out supporters of Chiang Kai-shek lined up on one side, Communists on the other side and nobody allowed in the middle. Independents like myself must be cleared out of the middle of the picture because we knew what we were talking about and because people had read our books and articles.[7]

Such men as Lattimore knew that between 1945 and 1949 the Nationalist government had been given, mainly by the United States, three billion dollars' worth of aid and that a large part of this had been squandered by the Chiang régime or had fallen into Communist hands. They believed too that, as a State Department White Paper had stated in 1949, the Nationalist government was "so inept, selfish, purblind, and faithless, as to be beyond resurrection."

It was in 1950 that the late Senator Patrick McCarran, Chairman of the Senate Judiciary Committee, established the Subcommittee on Internal Security which was to carry on the witch hunt begun by the Senate Investigating Subcommittee in 1947. 1950 was a year of sensational events. In February, Senator Joseph McCarthy, whom few outside of Wisconsin had ever heard of, burst into the limelight with the notorious speech in Wheeling, West Virginia, in which he said there were 205 Communists or fellow travelers in the State Department. In June, anti-Truman anti-Communists were somewhat embarrassed when the President sent American troops to Korea to help the South Koreans fight their Communist neighbors. They were relieved, however, when the Communist North Koreans were joined by "volunteers" from Communist China—that creation of the United States State Department, a creature that was now killing "our boys" in Korea. And their embarrassment ceased entirely when

[7] Owen Lattimore, *Ordeal by Slander*, Boston: Little, Brown and Co., 1954, p. 16.

Truman rebuked General Douglas MacArthur for carrying the pursuit of the enemy too far against orders from Washington and when the General was relieved of his command shortly thereafter.

Unconscious of the illogic of their views of this sequence of events, the China Lobby felt that it had a real cause. Accordingly, the lobby's senatorial agent, the McCarran committee, focused attention on an organization named the Institute of Pacific Relations which had performed signal services before and during World War II. This, it thought, was the true villain of the piece.

What the committee did then would have done credit to the most astute Soviet secret police bureau. It found a barn in Lee, Massachusetts, on the estate of an IPR administrator, in which were stored the records of the Institute, took possession of it, seized all the records and took them, in an armed convoy, to Washington. The committee then gave these to its extensive staff which studied them for five months. McCarran's reason for this was that Budenz and others had accused members of the Institute of subversive behavior and Senator McCarthy, now riding high on the crest of his new celebrity, had called its director, Owen Lattimore, "one of the top Communist agents in this country." Assuming Lattimore's guilt, the McCarran committee then built a case against him as formidable as any presented in the Stalin purges.

Many of the papers in the barn dealt with matters ten or more years old, many of them trivia which a man as busy as Lattimore had been could not remember. These, McCarran's prosecuting committee used with the definite intent, so Mr. Lattimore's lawyers believed, of trapping him into perjury. The questions were adroitly framed in advance. No careful reader of the hearings can doubt that the questions were designed not to elicit information but to catch the victim in a misstatement.

When Senator McCarthy's first charge was made, Mr. Lattimore was in Afghanistan where he headed a United Nations mission. He has written a moving account of the telegrams which came to him from the Associated Press asking for comment on the McCarthy accusation, of the letters from his wife confirming the charge, and of his return to the United States to prepare his defense.

In July, 1951, more than a year after McCarthy made his charge, the committee called Mr. Lattimore and interrogated him in executive session—that is, behind closed doors. The next steps, as recounted by his attorney, were these:

The Committee then went into open session and from July 25, 1951 to February 21, 1952 took eight volumes of testimony much of it attacking Mr. Lattimore in his absence but none of it given by him although he had asked to be heard. Finally, in February 1952 the Committee granted Mr. Lattimore's request for an opportunity to answer the charges which for months had been given wide publicity from the Committee forum.

After this period of character assassination by press and misinformed public opinion, the really grueling part of the ordeal began.

When at last Mr. Lattimore came to the stand for public hearings . . . the Committee kept him under cross-examination for twelve days, the longest interrogation of one man in Congressional history. The cross-examination encompassed the story of his life; his associations; his conversations, even the most casual; his conferences, public and private; and in the utmost detail his activities during a period of from ten to fifteen years from the early 1930's until by his own voluntary action he came to Washington from the center of Afghanistan to defend his loyalty and his good name before the Congress of his country.[8]

During these hearings, Lattimore was not permitted to refresh his memory by consulting any records, letters, diaries, or other

[8] U.S. District Court for the District of Columbia, U.S. v. Owen Lattimore. Memorandum in Support of Motion to Dismiss the Indictment. Action for Perjury under D.C. Code (22 D.C. Code 2501) Feb. 16, 1953, pp. 3, 4.

171

documents. The questions must be answered then and there with the knowledge that the Committee had the correct answers and could seize on any of its victim's lapses of memory. He was not, of course, permitted representation by counsel.

You will not be permitted [the Chairman told Lattimore's counsel, Mr. Abe Fortas] to testify and you will not be permitted to suggest answers to questions. When the witness seeks your counsel he will have opportunity to obtain your counsel.

Thank you, Senator [Mr. Fortas replied]. May I ask whether I am permitted to object to questions?

No, sir [replied the Chairman].[9]

At the start of these hearings, McCarran referred to a preliminary statement as being critical of his committee. Such criticism he said was a characteristic Communist tactic. In effect, therefore, he accused Lattimore of being a Communist, before the "defendant" had a chance to testify in his own behalf. These were his words:

Every Communist in America has taken opportunity to cast invective and discouraging and disparaging remarks with reference to this committee and its membership. We were fully advised before we undertook this task that such would be the course and procedure. It is not at all out of line with the general procedure of the Communist party and Communists generally in the world . . . A statement has been filed today by the witness. . . . The witness must be responsible for the full gravity of his remarks produced in that statement. *In that statement there is carried out the same policy as has been carried out against this committee. . . .* [Emphasis added.][1]

In such a prejudiced atmosphere the hearings continued. The witness was constantly interrupted in his answers to the ques-

[9] Hearings on the Institute of Pacific Relations before the Senate Internal Security Subcommittee (Feb. 26, 1952), part 9, p. 2898.
[1] *Ibid.*, pp. 2897–98.

tions put to him, his wording criticized, fault found with his refusal to answer yes or no to questions impossible so to answer and, in general, harassed in the Vishinsky manner. This, at any rate, is how the hearings impressed one member of the press who attended them.

> The hearing [wrote the representative of the *Washington Post*] conjured up images of ancient inquisitorial techniques and of the bludgeoning which is said to be the typical Soviet police method of eliciting information. But information was not the aim of this inquiry. It was hard to regard its aim as anything but sadistic.[2]

After four or five attempts to begin his statement, Mr. Lattimore was finally permitted to read its opening paragraph:

> The impression has been assiduously conveyed in your proceedings that I am a Communist or a Communist sympathizer or dupe; that I master-minded the Institute of Pacific Relations; that the Institute of Pacific Relations and I master-minded the Far Eastern experts of the State Department; and that the State Department "sold" China to the Russians. Every one of these is false—utterly and completely false.[3]

4

Before following these strange hearings to their conclusions it would be instructive to go back a year or so to discover what had happened in the Senate when Joseph McCarthy had first made his charge against Owen Lattimore. This will show that even the Senate of the Eighty-first Congress was not mainly composed of McCarthys and McCarrans or men of their stripe. If it were we might well despair of the republic's survival. But there are always responsible men in that upper chamber of our national legislature—men of learning, intelligence, and understanding—men

[2] Alan Barth, *Government by Investigation,* p. 102.
[3] Hearings, p. 2918.

who could remain sane even in the tornado of hysteria which swept Capitol Hill from 1950 until 1954.

Thus when Senator McCarthy had launched his indiscriminate charges in 1950 against many persons including Owen Lattimore, Philip Jessup, John Stewart Service, Esther Brunauer, Dorothy Kenyon, and John Carter Vincent, a subcommittee of the Senate Foreign Relations Committee was appointed with Senator Millard Tydings at its head to investigate the accusations. Tydings of Maryland had had a long and distinguished career in the Senate. With him were Theodore Green of Rhode Island and Brien McMahon of Connecticut. Dissident members were Bourke Hickenlooper of Iowa and Henry Cabot Lodge, Jr., of Massachusetts.

After four months of research through eighty-one State Department loyalty files and other material, the Committee presented its majority report which cleared Lattimore, Jessup, Service, Vincent, Mrs. Brunauer, and Judge Kenyon and called McCarthy's charges

a fraud and a hoax perpetrated on the Senate of the United States and the American people. They represent perhaps the most nefarious campaign of half-truths and untruth in the history of this Republic. For the first time in our history, we have seen the totalitarian technique of the "big lie" employed on a sustained basis. The result has been to confuse and divide the American people at a time when they should be strong in their unity.[4]

The report considered the effect of the unsupported charges on the fight against communism.

We sincerely believe that charges of the character which have been made in this case seriously impair the efforts of our agencies of Government to combat the problem of sub-

[4] The so-called Tydings Subcommittee of the Committee on Foreign Relations was appointed pursuant to Senate Resolution 231, 81st Cong., 2d Sess. Its report was Senate Report 2108, p. 167.

version. Furthermore, extravagant allegations, which cannot be proved and are not subject to proof, have the inevitable effect of dulling the awareness of all Americans to the true menace of communism. . . .

Communism represents the most diabolical concept ever designed to enslave mankind. Its stock and [sic] trade are deception, falsehood, and hate. The one hope of communism's success is to divide our people at home and our allies abroad. The false charges made in this case have succeeded in accomplishing to a great degree what the Communists themselves have been unable to do. These charges have created distrust and suspicion at home and raised serious doubts abroad.

We can never hope to preserve for posterity the American dream of freedom by adopting totalitarian methods as an excuse to preserve that freedom.[5]

Senators Hickenlooper and Lodge refused to sign the report, thus escaping the purge of Tydings, engineered by the vindictive McCarthy in the 1950 Congressional elections.[6]

It was not until the following year that McCarthy had fully consolidated his power. By that time the McCarran committee felt safe in the knowledge that the Senator from Wisconsin had scared too many members of the Senate to permit any effective resistance to its tactics. Also, the elimination of Tydings left it, so its members thought, free to ignore the report of his subcommittee. That report will, to be sure, make interesting reading for impartial historians in the future.

5

When the hearings of the McCarran committee ended, the chairman turned over its records to the Department of Justice. This resulted in the indictment of Lattimore for perjury on seven counts by a grand jury of the District of Columbia. The indict-

[5] *Ibid.*, p. 152.
[6] On the persecution of Tydings, called in the Senate "The Whitewash King," see 97 CR 1657 (Feb. 23, 1951).

ment stated that he had lied in denying certain charges. He had said:

> I have in fact been falsely identified as a fellow traveler, sympathizer, or follower of the Communist line or promoter of Communist interests . . . I am none of these things and never have been.

This constituted the first count. The others came from Lattimore's falling into traps set for him by the committee by questions about trivial incidents of fifteen or more years back. When the case came before the United States District Court for the District of Columbia, Judge Luther W. Youngdahl said:

> In the indictment under consideration, defendant is not charged with lying in denying that he was a Communist or a member of the Communist Party. The indictment here charges defendant with committing perjury as to his sympathies with communism or Communist interests (count one); whether he had been told or knew certain persons were Communists (counts two and three); whether he had published certain articles in "Pacific Affairs" by Communists (count four); whether he had a lunch engagement with Soviet Ambassador Oumansky in July, 1941 after the Hitler invasion (count five); that he did not at the request of Lauchlin Currie take care of his mail at the White House (count six); and whether he had made pre-arrangements with the Communist Party to get into Yenan (count seven).
>
> It appears from the record and the hearings of the Committee that the charges reflected in the seven counts in the indictment related to a period of fifteen to twenty years before the hearings . . .
>
> Aside from the reasons of invalidity as to certain counts as hereinafter expressed, there is serious doubt in the Court's mind whether any count in this indictment can finally pass the test of materiality.[7]

[7] U.S. v. Lattimore., Cr. No. 1879-52, U.S. District Court, District of Columbia, May 2, 1953. Federal Supplement vol. 112, pp. 511, 513.

Summarily, the judge dismissed the first count as "fatally defective." He said, too, that the count was "violative of the Sixth Amendment, which protects the accused in the right to be informed of the nature and cause of the accusation against him." Eventually all the charges were dismissed as being "formless and obscure" and Lattimore was never brought to trial. Yet the unhappy professor had been put through some five years of anguish by the irresponsible conduct of a group of legislators probably motivated—as Senator McCarthy was—by political ambitions.

No man [wrote Elmer Davis in *But We Were Born Free*] has ever been more relentlessly persecuted by a Congressional committee than Owen Lattimore by the Internal Security Committee under Senator McCarran.[8]

The effect of this interlude of dictated injustice is, however, more far-reaching than any distress it may have caused any individual. It has established a precedent by which men sworn to uphold the Constitution have, under the pretense of emergency, nullified certain of its provisions. It has established a precedent by which the equivalent of a Bill of Attainder—that anathema of the Founding Fathers—may be passed against a citizen. It has put a stamp of approval by the top legislative chamber of the country on a total alteration of the function of Congressional committees of investigation. And it has drawn a blueprint for the dissemination of unreasonable and panic fears among the people that may be used at any future moment in the complex and difficult years ahead.

6

Egged on by the China Lobby, McCarthy went on to a point that has since been condemned by many who were then his supporters. Perhaps he went further than even the extremists of this cause would have dared go. Undoubtedly it was one of the rea-

[8] Elmer Davis, *But We Were Born Free*, Indianapolis: Bobbs Merrill Co., 1954, p. 65.

sons for his decline. Yet while he exploited his fantasies, he did great damage not only to the target of his attack but to the reputation of a President of the United States who, in the course of a political campaign, was intimidated into turning his back on a friend.

General George Catlett Marshall was a hero second only to Eisenhower in popular esteem. Many close students of the second World War even thought him a greater strategist than Eisenhower. While Eisenhower was in command in Europe, Marshall was concerned also in the Pacific. Indeed, it was his concern in the Orient that got him into trouble.

McCarthy, who was not always distinguished by elegance of expression, called Marshall a "sacred cow." It was not hard, he explained, to expose subversive persons such as Hiss or Harry White but "the difficult task, the unpleasant task, is to dig out the sacred cows."[9] In the case of Marshall, he conquered his distaste, and wrote a speech 60,000 words long, accusing the General of having betrayed the Chinese Nationalists into the hands of the Chinese Communists and of having assured Communist control of all China with the result that "our boys" bled and died in Korea. He preceded this final charge by giving a history of Marshall's conduct during the war, alleging that the General had consistently opposed Churchill and other allied strategists because of his desire to help Russia. This lengthy biography was designed to show that Marshall had always been pro-Communist.[1] The Senator had thought it necessary to give this detailed proof because he had previously been questioned on the floor of the Senate by those few Senators who by 1951 were still brave enough to question him.

Senator Morse, of Oregon, for instance, had expressed doubts in March when McCarthy was launching some trial balloons on the subject.

[9] 97 CR 2391, 2392 (Mar. 14, 1951).
[1] 97 CR 6556-6603 (June 14, 1951). This was later made into a book, *Retreat from Victory: The Story of George C. Marshall*, privately printed, 1952.

178

I have [said Morse] a little difficulty in reconciling my thinking with any implication that General Marshall is pro-Communist, when I think of the stand which he takes as Secretary
of Defense, in opposition to everything that is Communist, and
the warnings that he gives us on the Armed Services Committee, that if we do not strengthen ourselves to a position of maximum security, we run the risk of losing our security from
Communist aggression . . . I have great difficulty in believing
that General Marshall does not hate communism just as much
as does the Senator from Wisconsin . . .[2]

McCarthy then hedged slightly saying that Marshall acted on
orders from the State Department, notably Secretary Acheson
and the "Acheson-Hiss-Yalta" crowd, thus reassuring those Republican colleagues who hated the party in power far worse than
they hated Communists, that he was motivated primarily by
partisan impulses.

If the General was hurt by this attack from the Senate, it could
have been nothing compared with the pain he must have suffered
when his greatest friend, Dwight Eisenhower, was so intimidated
by the followers of McCarthy that, on the occasion of his visit to
Wisconsin during his campaign for the presidency in 1952, he
was persuaded to omit in the speech he delivered there a tribute
to Marshall. The passage was in his written speech; undoubtedly
he had put it there because of the irresponsible attacks in the
Senate; but he was persuaded to blue-pencil it by the Wisconsin
politicians. It is, perhaps, the most shameful incident in the life
of a great general and a great American hero.

The whole affair has tragic aspects. One is the disillusionment
which seems always to follow a war, even a victorious one. In the
early 1950's there was doubt among many Americans as to
whether we had really won the war; doubt as to whether we had
defeated the real enemy; doubt whether any of it was worth
while; fear lest we should have it to do all over again. This is
appropriate weather for the demagogue to make hay. He can tell

[2] 97 CR 2892 (Mar. 14, 1951).

us that we really lost the war after all, and most effective of all, he can provide us with scapegoats.

The Russian Communists must have taken pleasure in the split in the American people produced by the Senate's wedge. They must have watched with enjoyment the split it produced between the United States and its allies. They certainly profited by the respite that came to them when Americans turned from fighting them to fighting each other. These results they never could have attained through their agents, their spies, their saboteurs. But most important of all that barking down the wrong trails of the Congressional bloodhounds provided cover for the real spies.

That is the pity of those years.

XII. The New Broom

IF THE Tydings subcommittee can be accused of "whitewashing" Owen Lattimore, the McCarran subcommittee may well be charged with brainwashing him. Except for the glaring lights under which Communist victims are interrogated in Moscow, the procedure in the case of Lattimore was much the same as in Russia. Whether or not the McCarran staff had done research in Soviet methods before the hearings began, they gave an excellent imitation of them. The difference, however, between such methods in the totalitarian Soviet Union and in the democratic United States lies in the role of the press and press-actuated public opinion in the two countries. In Russia, where the press is rigidly controlled, brainwashing is not reported in detail because it is unnecessary for the public to know about it. Public opinion there is unimportant. In the United States, however, where public opinion affects Congressional and governmental exercise, the press becomes a vital though sometimes unintentional instrument for turning an unfavorable public light upon the victim of a Congressional investigating committee. The American press thus adds to the stigma put upon him by the investigators.

The other principal difference in the results of Soviet and American brainwashing is that the Congressional variety is seldom wholly successful. Americans, no matter what ordeal they may have suffered, do not confess to guilt of which they are innocent. Their brains, in short, are not washed clean. The "defendants" may be tricked into false testimony so that they land in jail, convicted of perjury, but they do not break down in simulated penitence with the hope of avoiding the gallows—whose shadow, as yet, does not fall upon them. All they have to lose is reputation and the chance to earn their living.

In 1952 when, through the efforts of the anti-Democrat anti-Communists, several persons were in jail and others on the threshold, Dwight Eisenhower who, four years before had stated that presidential candidates should not be drawn from the military, forgot his general's stars and let himself be nominated by the Republican Party. There was an exciting Republican national convention in which the delegates turned from fighting Democrats to fighting each other. The bitterness of the conflict between the supporters of Senator Robert Taft and those of General Dwight Eisenhower replaced the usual inter-party rancor. Nor did it subside when Eisenhower won and it was said that, as the election approached, certain Taft supporters hoped for a Democratic victory.

The moment Eisenhower's face appeared on the television screens, however, he was elected. The balloting in November was the merest formality. The public forgot its postwar disillusionment, decided that the war had really been won, after all, and that Eisenhower had, personally, won it. He had saved the country. Now it would remain safe in his hands. Now he would end the Korean war which the Democrats had lost anyway but which was continuing in a desultory fashion, keeping our boys away from home and, indeed, often killing them. The General promised to go, himself, in the flesh, to Korea, and obviously the mere appearance there of a great general would cause an immediate cease-fire and eventual peace.

But there was more to it than that. There was his genial smile, his comforting words, and especially, his obvious ignorance of politics. We were sick of politics. In times like these after years of wrangling in the Congress and between legislative and executive branches, the American people often searches for an amateur. Such a man would be "clean," uncorrupted, above all the petty squabbles that diverted legislators and bureaucrats alike from orderly governmental processes. And, with the Congressional Republican victories certain to accompany the Republican presidential victory, there would be a new broom in Washington. The "thievery in high places" that had "characterized" the Truman administration would be gone forever. So even long-time Democrats voted for Ike.

A few long-time Republicans noted that the campaign was not wholly clean. As election day neared, for example, the irrepressible McCarthy delivered an attack on the Democratic candidate, Adlai Stevenson, in which the Senator spoke of the Communist influences with which Stevenson was supposed to be surrounded.

Tonight, [he said] I shall give you the history of the Democrat candidate . . . who endorses and would continue the suicidal Kremlin-shaped policies of this nation.

The fabric of lies that followed must have embarrassed a good many Republican listeners. But when, McCarthy said, working up to a resounding climax, we get a Republican administration and Congress,

we will have the power to help Dwight Eisenhower scrub and flush and wash clean the foul mess of corruption and Communism in Washington.[1]

Elmer Davis, the news commentator, who maintained that McCarthy's television time "was paid for largely by the old America First crowd," later wrote,

When I listened to that broadcast . . . I was reminded of another rabble-rousing broadcaster in another republic, who was taken up by rich men and conservative politicians because they

[1] Radio-TV Broadcast, Chicago, Oct. 27, 1952, from "McCarthy Broadcast Dinner," a $50 a plate dinner in the grand ballroom of the Palmer House. The dinner was arranged by Gen. Robert C. Wood, board chairman, of Sears, Roebuck & Co., formerly prominent in "America First" 1940, 1941. *New York Times*, Oct. 28, 1952, gives full text on p. 26.

183

thought they could use his talent for publicity . . . When I heard the applause for McCarthy that night an echo of memory seemed to give it an undertone—*Sieg Heil! Sieg Heil! Sieg Heil.*[2]

2

When the new President was inaugurated in January, 1953, and his new cabinet installed, the new Attorney General set about the washing, scrubbing, and flushing that McCarthy had prophesied. All the dirt that had accumulated in the dark corners of executive departments and bureaus must be swept out. The sweeping would have a dual result: it would leave Washington sweet and fresh for the prospective march of progress and it would give Congressional investigating committees as well as the Department of Justice something to do.

The Committees were hungry for new victims. Representative Harold Velde of Illinois, formerly employed by the FBI, now headed the House Committee on Un-American Activities and Senator William E. Jenner of Indiana took over the Internal Security Subcommittee. McCarthy had his own private instrument of torture, the Permanent Subcommittee on Investigations of the Committee on Government Operations—a group which, unfortunately for the Wisconsin Senator's supporters, contained the seeds of his own destruction.

Mr. Herbert Brownell, the new vacuum-cleaning Attorney General, and Mr. J. Edgar Hoover started an immediate combing of the FBI files in their search for persons who had assisted the treason of the Truman administration. They came up with something quite sensational. The subject, in this case, could no longer be brainwashed or defend himself, since he was dead, but he provided an excellent case against the Truman administration which, in the opinion of zealous Republicans, had nurtured a spy in its bosom.

The case of Harry Dexter White, which Brownell and Hoover exhumed in 1953, had been thoroughly thrashed out and had

[2] Davis, *op. cit.*, p. 93.

received, one would think, a proper burial, along with its subject, some five years before. In 1947, the Department of Justice had presented the FBI dossier on White to a grand jury. After White had given the jury his private testimony in which he denied any connection with the Communist Party, the jury declined to indict on the ground of insufficient evidence. The following year, the House Un-American Activities Committee held its celebrated session in which Whittaker Chambers testified against Alger Hiss. Both he and Elizabeth Bentley included White among those whom they accused of espionage.

White was suffering at the time from a severe heart ailment. Nevertheless, he appeared, between heart attacks, before the House committee, frankly and fearlessly answered all the questions put to him, vigorously denied the charges, and asserted his complete innocence. The record of those hearings makes an illuminating exhibit for the annals of man's inhumanity to man. Doubt was even cast on his heart condition when he told of his fondness for Ping-pong—a game he admitted he had played with another suspect.

At the start of this hearing, he had sent the committee's chairman, J. Parnell Thomas, a private note, explaining his condition and asking for an occasional recess. Here is the dialogue between the chairman and Witness White:

MR. WHITE: Yes, I was at the [Silvermaster] basement. It was at a party, and they were playing Ping-pong. I fancied myself a little as a Ping-pong player, and we played a few times.

THE CHAIRMAN: Just a minute right there. Let me see that note. One thing I cannot reconcile, Mr. White, you send me a note and you say that "I am recovering from a severe heart attack. I would appreciate it if the chairman would give me five or ten minutes rest after each hour." For a person who had a severe heart condition, you certainly play a lot of sports.

MR. WHITE: I did not intend that this note should be read aloud. I do not know any reason why it should be public that I am ill, but I think probably one of the reasons why I suffered

185

a heart attack was because I played so many sports and so well. The heart attack which I suffered was last year. I am speaking of playing Ping-pong, and I was a fair tennis player, and a pretty good ball player, many years prior to that. I hope that clears that up, Mr. Chairman.[3]

Two days after the close of the hearing, Harry Dexter White died. Mr. Thomas must have been distressed by such an interruption to his inquisition. But his committee at the time was in a frenzy of excitement over the disclosures of David Whittaker Chambers, ex-Communist spy, about Alger Hiss, and were willing enough to let the revelations about White follow him into the grave.

3

The Harry White scandal was, however, too potent politically to be allowed to rest in a cemetery. In 1953, therefore, in the midst of the great new house-cleaning, it was dug up and paraded through the nation with maximum publicity. It was important, then, to show that the previous Democratic administration had swarmed with traitors; that this new immaculate executive had thus inherited a series of extremely difficult problems and that the cleaning-out of the departmental stables was a task before which Hercules himself would hesitate. There was, moreover, a practical purpose. In several states there would be close contests in November over gubernatorial elections and it was incumbent upon zealous Republicans to show how corrupt Democrats could be.

This is the only rational explanation for the exhuming of the unhappy White. It is true that the FBI and investigating committees had turned up other villains. But that so special an emphasis should be put on the behavior of a man five years dead against whom only vague and unsubstantiated charges had been

[3] Hearings regarding Communist Espionage in the U.S. Government before House Committee to Investigate Un-American Activities, 80th Cong., 2d Sess., p. 881 (Aug. 13, 1948).

brought suggested to the unprejudiced observer that the Attorney General and the august Senate were wasting their time, not to mention the taxpayers' money.

But this whole new post-mortem investigation seemed to Jenner and other anti-liberals in the Senate desirable in more ways than one. It would enable the Subcommittee on Internal Security to carry on under Senator Jenner the highly successful work of McCarran in the pillorying of Owen Lattimore. Also, it would steal part of the show from McCarthy, whose "permanent" subcommittee was getting all the headlines. Finally, it would focus the spotlight on Mr. Herbert Brownell, the most co-operative attorney general since Mitchell Palmer.

In April, 1953, the hearings of Senator Jenner's committee began. For the most part they centered in the testimony of Elizabeth Bentley, ex-Communist secret agent and spy. Ever since 1948, she had been telling about the "ring" of spies in the executive branch of the government. Out of her testimony, Jenner fabricated a pattern of "interlocking subversives" who helped one another get "sensitive" jobs, promoted one another, raised one another's salaries and were, in general, such good friends that they were always visiting at one another's homes and—this seemed to the Senate most damning of all—played volleyball and handball together.

But Harry Dexter White had been the key man. How do you know, Senator? Because the FBI has told Attorney General Brownell all about it. But the FBI files are secret. They cannot be made public. We must take Mr. Brownell's word. Obviously, he would not say so if it were not true.

The hearings went on into the summer. The committee's report was filed July 30. It was printed early in August and released to the press on August 24. It was immediately given wide circulation. Mr. David Lawrence, who has rarely shown fervent opposition to the Republican party or to McCarthy and other spy-hunters, printed it in full with many explanatory footnotes in the September 4 issue of his *U.S. News and World Report*. According to journalist Dan Gillmor:

187

Members of the Republican National Committee were so impressed that they arranged for the purchase of extra copies to be placed in the hands of Party workers in states where close gubernatorial races were slated for November. A Texas multi-millionaire and heavy financial backer of both Senators McCarthy and Jenner in 1952 patriotically paid for 50,000 more.[4]

The Committee's report is a masterpiece of selective skill and testifies to the remarkable editorial adroitness of the Brownell-Jenner axis and its staff. Mr. Gillmor's analysis of it to which he devotes two chapters of his book is well worth reading. It purports (among other things) to reproduce what it regards as the significant portions of the 1948 hearings before the House Committee on Un-American Activities when the suspected spies or espionage agents—White, Silverman, Silvermaster, Perlo, Coe et al.,—were interrogated by the committee's professional inquisitor, Robert Stripling.

In this reproduction stress is laid on the use of the Fifth Amendment by unfriendly witnesses, especially those who were already branded as Communists, their agents, or their spies. But no distinction was made between the use of the amendment on advice of counsel to conform to the "doctrine of waiver" and the firm denials by those same witnesses of criminal conduct.[5] The report simply stated that all the accused witnesses had invoked the Fifth Amendment to answer questions regarding Communist membership. Naturally. Such membership was not a crime. Had they answered these questions, they would have been required to answer other questions involving lists of names of their possibly quite innocent friends. So, though most of the accused witnesses did use the privilege for a part of their answers, they made flat denials of other direct or implied charges. The astute editors of the report discreetly omitted these denials, giving the impression that all had always taken refuge in the amendment.

[4] Dan Gillmor, *Fear, the Accuser*, New York: Abelard-Schuman Ltd., 1954, pp. 211–12. *The Reporter*, Dec. 22, 1953, pp. 9–12.
[5] For an explanation of the "doctrine of waiver" see pp. 88–89 *supra*.

A pointed passage showing the distinction between answers to questions involving criminal activity and those related to party membership was the dialogue between the House Committee's clever staff investigator Robert Stripling and William Ludwig Ullmann.

MR. STRIPLING: Did you ever furnish any information to Nathan Gregory Silvermaster obtained in your official capacity in the Army?

MR. ULLMANN: No.

MR. STRIPLING: Are you a member of the Communist Party?

MR. ULLMANN: I refuse to answer that question on the ground that it might tend to incriminate me.

MR. STRIPLING: Do you know Elizabeth Bentley?

MR. ULLMANN: I refuse to answer . . .

MR. STRIPLING: Did you ever furnish any information to Elizabeth T. Bentley?

MR. ULLMANN: No.[6]

Yet, in the Jenner report, Brownell listed Ullmann as one of those "who claimed their privilege not to answer questions. . . ," implying that the witness refused to answer all questions. Again, the editors of the report blue-penciled the dialogue between A. George Silverman (not to be confused with Silvermaster) and committeeman F. Edward Hébert of Louisiana.

MR. HEBERT: You face your accuser, [Elizabeth Bentley] Dr. Silverman. What is your answer? Is she telling the truth, or isn't she telling the truth, and do you recognize her?

MR. SILVERMAN: In my opinion, she is telling a huge web of lies.

[6] Espionage in U.S. Government Hearings (1948), p. 745.

MR. HEBERT: You tell Miss Bentley here—that is contrary to the fact that you refused to answer because it might incriminate you. Are you waiving that now?

MR. SILVERMAN: With respect to the charge of espionage and any other criminal conduct, I waive.[7]

The report does not refer to Silverman's waiver. Perhaps the Attorney General did not want to open any discussion of the legal technicalities here involved. To the average layman, the invocation of the Fifth Amendment is indicative of guilt. For the purposes of the report, it was discreet not to interfere with any such illusion.

4

The really shocking hearings, however, Brownell persuaded the committee to reserve for the autumn. Perhaps it was a coincidence that the Attorney General's most devastating speech was made just before certain November elections. To the Chicago Executives Club on November 6, he said:

Harry Dexter White was a Russian spy. He . . . was known to be a Communist spy by the very people who appointed him to the most sensitive and important post he ever held in government service.[8]

This remarkable statement by a lawyer committed to the presumption that a person is innocent until he is proved guilty suggested that he must possess some extremely conclusive evidence. To those not knowledgeable about jurisprudence in a free democracy, the speech was an assurance that White's guilt had been proved.

The Attorney General later said definitely that by "the very people who appointed him" he meant President Truman.

[7] *Ibid.*, p. 847.
[8] *New York Times*, Nov. 7, p. 1, col. 8.

Throughout Mr. Brownell's melodrama, he made it clear that Truman was the bull's-eye of his target.

Having delivered his shocker in Chicago in the nick of time for its political effect, Mr. Brownell felt it incumbent upon him to produce his proof. Meanwhile he assured Director J. Edgar Hoover that he would take the responsibility for divulging excerpts from the confidential files of the FBI by "declassifying" this material, thus rendering it no longer secret.

Mr. Brownell and Senator Jenner were both showmen of uncommon ability. They were determined that the supplementary hearings which were to bolster the report on Interlocking Subversives be presented to the people in the most dramatic way. They therefore arranged for the hearings to be televised. This would enable the Attorney General to stand in the foreground alongside the Number One American hero, J. Edgar Hoover himself.

> This afternoon, I want to discuss [said Mr. Brownell as the first act opened] the case of Harry Dexter White and the manner in which it was handled by the Truman administration on the basis of established facts and the records in the Department of Justice.[9]

Having thus proclaimed to the several million viewers the strictly partisan intent of the hearings, the Attorney General went on.

> The letter I hold in my hand [he continued, borrowing the familiar McCarthy phraseology] is marked "Top Secret." I have declassified it and will make it public because it does not reveal any security information which would now be damaging . . .[1]

The letter, signed by J. Edgar Hoover, was addressed to Brigadier General Harry Hawkins Vaughan, Military Aide to the

[9] Interlocking Subversion in Government Departments. Hearings before the Subcommittee on Internal Security. Part 16, p. 1111.
[1] *Ibid.*, p. 1113.

President. It was dated November 8, 1945, and was inscribed "Top secret by Special messenger" and directed to the White House. It told General Vaughan that

> As a result of the Bureau's investigative operations, information has been recently developed from *a highly confidential source* indicating that a number of persons employed by the Government of the United States have been furnishing data to persons outside the Federal Government, who are in turn transmitting this information to espionage agents of the Soviet Government. At the present time *it is impossible to determine exactly how many of these people had actual knowledge of the disposition being made of the information they were transmitting.* The investigation, however, at this point has indicated that the persons named hereafter were actually the source from which information passing through the Soviet espionage system was being obtained. . . . [Emphasis added.][2]

While this letter could be declassified by Mr. Brownell, the "confidential" source of the information could not. Therefore, it was not possible to know whether the persons named were "conscious" traitors or not.

Thirteen persons were named, the most important of whom were White, Lauchlin Currie, former administrative assistant to Franklin Roosevelt, five employees of the Office of Strategic Services (OSS), an army colonel, and an air force captain. The letter added that Mary Price, former secretary to Walter Lippmann and later manager of a CIO organization, would maybe soon join the suspects.

This, Mr. Brownell insisted, was preliminary. He then introduced a later letter, Hoover to Vaughan, stating that

> . . . Information has come to the attention of this Bureau charging White as being a valuable adjunct to an underground Soviet espionage organization operating in Washington, D. C. . . .[3]

[2] *Ibid.*
[3] *Ibid.*, p. 1115.

Again the "confidential" source of the information was not disclosed. The letter goes on to tell what White did, using his employees (also listed in the earlier letter as suspects), but it is careful to state that he "allegedly" did these things. It did name the Russian recipients of the material said to be passed through White and these included Jacob Golos, Miss Bentley's former boy friend—so the circle appeared closed.

It is safe to conclude that such evidence with its vagueness, its allusion to mysterious confidential sources, and the obvious caution with which it was presented, would hardly have been accepted in a court of law over the objections of defense counsel. Counsel would not only have insisted on the identification of the source, but would also insist that, under the provisions of the Sixth Amendment to the Constitution, the source be produced so that the defendant could confront him. House and Senate investigating committees, however, are rarely concerned with the Constitution or its Bill of Rights. In this case, the Jenner committee did all that it thought necessary; it persuaded many persons through their TV screens that a Democratic president had *consciously employed Russian spies in his executive departments.* These viewers were ignorant of judicial procedure, and as far as they are concerned communications from the FBI are, on the face of them, damning. Such was the effect of the publicity build-up achieved over the years by J. Edgar Hoover.

In fairness to Mr. Hoover, it may be said that he acted under orders of his boss, and that he was probably uncomfortable during the hearings. The letters, after all, had been written before the investigation was complete; they were intended chiefly as advices to be careful, and they were certainly never meant to provide lines for a theatrical production. He even admitted that his Bureau had been opposed to actual prosecution of White on the basis of its information in 1945 and 1946 because "some of the evidence, while of an irrefutable nature, was not admissible in a court of law."

Lest such admissions and other doubts becloud the viewers' view of the issue, Chairman Jenner elaborated on the Hoover

193

reports and summarized the documents according to his own interpretations.

Harry Dexter White [he concluded] was at the center of all this activity. His name was used for reference by other members of the ring, when they made applications for Federal employment. He hired them. He promoted them. He raised their salaries. He transferred them from bureau to bureau, from department to department. He assigned them to international missions. He vouched for their loyalty and protected them when exposure threatened. He played handball with them.[4]

This last grim accusation seems, as we read the statement, something of an anticlimax. To the Senator, however, it was probably a final proof of guilt by association—as if guilt had come off these subversive players' hands, got on the ball and was thus transferred, like bacteria, to the hands of Harry White.

5

Although these revelations were designed to shock, and probably did shock, most of the millions who followed them on their screens, the Attorney General had not yet played his trump card. This consisted in photostats of papers produced from Whittaker Chambers's pumpkin along with the damning copies of those of Alger Hiss. They were in White's handwriting. Chambers had produced them when White, being dead, could no longer explain where they came from or how they got into the collection known as the pumpkin papers. They had already been seen by the House Committee and noted in the espionage hearings of 1948 and they had been recorded in the *Congressional Record* in 1950. But they had been overshadowed by the Hiss documents. Now they were introduced into the posthumous trial of Harry White.

To conclude that the notes themselves were calculated to convey vital information to the Russians would require the exercise

[4] *Ibid.*, p. 1150 (Nov. 17, 1953).

of a highly creative imagination, though even then only a guess could be made at the means by which they got to Chambers.

That, indeed, thought persons unfriendly to the Jenner committee, was the missing link. Neither Brownell nor Hoover could produce evidence showing that White had given Chambers the papers or delivered them to him by any specified means.

> The documents [wrote the unfriendly correspondent of the *Washington Post*] may have been stolen from White or passed by him innocently to someone who gave them to Chambers . . .[5]

A less confident man than Attorney General Brownell might have been embarrassed by such a loose end. He might also have been embarrassed by the persistent inquiry: Why, if all this was true of White, had not a grand jury indicted him? Brownell's answer to this was that such a grand jury would certainly have done so had all the evidence been admissible to it. Unfortunately as Brownell admitted in the hearing much of it was in the form of transcriptions from the wire-tapping of telephone conversations. Federal courts had decided that evidence obtained by such invasion of privacy could not be introduced.[6]

When the hearings ended, then, nothing very definite had been accomplished. A dead man's name had been besmirched and several survivors had lost their jobs. No currently operating spies were caught by the investigation. The only residue from the whole affair was an evanescent glory for the Attorney General and some notoriety for Senator Jenner which, however, was soon dimmed by McCarthy's more glaring light.

It is a curious fact that none of the persons in the long list sent by Mr. Hoover to General Vaughan was ever convicted of anything in a court of law. Indeed, these persons accused by the Federal police bureau and by the Department of Justice of

---

[5] Alan Barth, *Government by Investigation*, p. 92.

[6] White was posthumously tried and convicted by *Time*, the weekly newsmagazine, in a "cover story," Nov. 23, 1953, of which its staff could scarcely have been proud. Presumably, however, it was *Time*'s duty to support its editor, former Communist spy, David Whittaker Chambers.

acts of disloyalty, betrayal, and espionage, of giving classified information to agents of a foreign government and of subverting government departments and bureaus, were never even indicted. No grand jury would concede that there was sufficient evidence for an indictment. Yet those who survived were duly punished. A committee responsible to the Senate of the United States had brought the equivalent of bills of attainder against them.

6

Of course the Soviets have spies in the United States. A number of Russian spies have been caught after extremely skillful work by the FBI, assisted by state and local police. They have been indicted, convicted, and sentenced in courts of law. It is probable that many others would have been discovered and punished but for the diversions practiced by Congressional committees or by Attorneys General with partisan political motives, who were bemused by klieg lights and television cameras. If the FBI were left alone to do its proper job, it would do a good one, but when it is dragged into committee hearings and its incomplete and unevaluated files exposed to public view—perhaps in the very midst of some hot pursuit—there is a chance the real criminals will escape.

In both Senate and House there are fine, incorruptible legislators. Such persons are probably in the majority at both ends of the Capitol. But there are also persons of easy political virtue as well as outright scoundrels, and to them the temptation to turn a partisan trick by accusing someone of subversive or un-American conduct is irresistible. It must be so in any parliament whose members are dependent on popular support by a partially ignorant electorate.

Fortunately the Founding Fathers were aware of precisely this temptation and our Constitution reflects their awareness. It provides checks and balances which have acted in many historical crises to keep equilibrium.

Unhappily, in these later days, communism has tipped the scale. Our obsession with it has caused the perversion of the

Founding Fathers' intent. It has given the Congress powers which the Constitution denies it; among them the power to attaint and punish individual citizens. The fear of communism has caused Congress and the Justice Department to elevate security above justice.

There are reasons for us to hate communism and to fight it. But our gun emplacements must be in the fortress our Fathers built for us; a fortress built of liberty, equality, and the rights of man. And we must aim our fire at communism's center, not at its foggy periphery.

XIII. Sixth Column South

THE INCREASINGLY ACCEPTED DOCTRINE that any person or group that one dislikes or disagrees with is Communist reached its peak in the deep South of the United States when Negroes assembled to promote enforcement of what they considered to be their civil rights. In the wake of the decision of the Supreme Court of the United States in 1954 that segregation in the public schools is unconstitutional, southern demagogues and rabble-rousers thought it justifiable to use any means at hand to defeat the aims of the Negroes and uphold white supremacy. As usual, the most convenient means was to pin the label of "Communist" upon those who sought redress for their grievances.

The Civil War, which has never quite ended in the United States, was stimulated to new energy by the Court's decision. The war was, to be sure, no longer fought on bloody battlefields, but its conflicts in the halls of Congress and in Federal courts were as bitter as they were indecisive. There were persons in the North as well as in the South who felt that it was difficult, if not impossible, to legislate against custom, and who sympathized with the way of life cherished by champions of the old South. There were many persons in the South as well as in the North who believed that segregation was a wholly undemocratic custom and that, in the Nation's maturity, Jim Crow laws had become obsolete. Thus, the Civil War in its new form no longer respects geographical limits.

The racial issue has, of course, run parallel with the history of the United States. For most of the first century of that history, it

198

had a specific focus: Negro slavery. Into the circle of that focus were drawn the moral, economic, and legal factors in the issue. After the Emancipation Proclamation and the Constitutional amendments consequent upon it, the focus was diffused. In the years that followed the War Between the States the emphasis has become increasingly political: the main question was whether the Negro could actually enjoy the civil rights guaranteed him by the amended Constitution. Those Southerners who remained nostalgic for the old plantation way of life, gone with the wind as it might be, wanted to deny the Negro those rights—by illegal means if necessary. In the southland, nullification was not a new exercise.

When the Supreme Court, after much backing and filling, finally decided against discrimination, it was a distressing blow to Southern nostalgists. To them the law of the land seemed to have declared itself against custom. The shock of a decree which should send their children to schools in which they must sit cheek by jowl with black children, whose backwardness had been a product of segregation, was violent indeed.

The decision naturally stimulated the Negroes to new endeavors. Although for many decades, they had been working and hoping for approach to equality—at least political if not economic and social equality to white citizens—they now saw, for the first time, light at the end of their tunnel of misery, and they were determined through their organization, the National Association for the Advancement of Colored People, to take advantage of their gain and push for desegregation.

To secure this in the schools they brought suits against the school boards which had excluded colored children and, in many cases, they were successful in establishing a degree of integration in the institutions of higher education and token integration in several elementary schools.

They did not, however, stop at that. Their aim was to break the Jim Crow restrictions in public transportation, as well as in public facilities in station waiting rooms and restaurants and at the lunch counters where Negroes were forced to stand while

199

white patrons sat—a rule which seemed even to those Northerners who favored other practices of segregation, the ultimate in
absurdity. To accomplish these things, they brought economic
pressures through boycotts and staged sit-down strikes which
greatly harassed the police in southern cities. They were, however, surprisingly successful even in the deep South. As a climax
to these activities they sent so-called "freedom riders" in char-
tered buses through southern territory, defying the police and
provoking arrest.

There was nothing new in all this activity. Not only in
the United States but in various nations of the free world,
labor organizations, organized pacifists, "suffragettes," political
or economic pickets had done similar things to arouse sympathetic public opinion. It was inevitable that, in the course of
such proceedings, however much the leaders might warn against
it, sporadic violence would break out. In the conflict between
whites and Negroes in the South, there were acts on both sides
that were bloody and destructive. Nor were these outbreaks
confined to the South; there were race riots in such northern industrial cities as Detroit and Cleveland.

Organized racial demonstrations were so natural that a search
for external subversion seems superfluous. Of course the Negroes
had grievances, severe grievances, grievances of long standing.
In a democracy nothing was more normal than that they should
take advantage of the right guaranteed them in the First Amendment to organize and assemble in the interest of redress. In
late years, however, it has become fashionable to assume that
any demonstration or protest against any law, economic condition or social custom, however unjust, must have been inspired
by the universal enemy, the Communist Party. So when this
fashion took hold in the Congress, it gave the Senators and
Representatives from Dixie their great opportunity. If they could
accuse Negro leaders of being Communists; if they could imply
that the National Association for the Advancement of Colored
People had been "infiltrated" by radical subversives—they could
persuade other legislators to point fingers of contempt at all

Negro protests. Thus, across the Mason and Dixon line, a new
Sixth Column was born.

Southerners, though they have been accused of it by rabid
Northern promoters of the new civil war, do not hate the dark
race. On the contrary, their affection for colored individuals is
proverbial. It endures until the black man uses the white man's
devices to lift himself to the white man's level. As one Virginian
once eloquently if inelegantly expressed it: "I hate Negroes, but
I love niggers." Actually, true racial hatred is probably nearly
as prevalent in the North as in the South. In many Northern
cities racial discrimination is often brutal indeed. But what the
white-supremacy Southerner truly hates is organization. He
hates the National Association for the Advancement of Colored
People. He is happy to think of it as a "Communist front." One
wag of the deep South called it the National Association for
the Advancement of the Communist Party.

Intelligent and enlightened Southerners, of whom the number
is constantly growing even in the most intolerant areas, know
better. They know that the conflict between this dominant Negro
organization and the Communist Party has been long and bitter. They know that the average Negro has been quick to see
through the fraud and the hoax that Communists have tried to
trick him into or, if he is inarticulate about the trickery, feels
an instinctive repulsion for communism and all its works. But
especially they know that the NAACP is one of the strongest
anti-Communist organizations in the country. Unfortunately,
however, most senators and congressmen from the southern
states do not belong to the intelligent and enlightened group.

2

Nevertheless, the suspicion that the NAACP is Communist-
dominated is not implausible. From the start, it has been a
principal aim of the Party to recruit Negroes to its support. It
has used every trick in its bag. Through deceit it has formed
"fronts"—Negro organizations which dissolved as soon as their
members became aware that they had been deceived. It has

201

made constant efforts to infiltrate the NAACP. But, as Wilson Record, Assistant Professor of Sociology at San Francisco State College, writes:

> Should the Party succeed in its present efforts to penetrate the NAACP, for example, it is highly probable that the latter would disintegrate in much the same manner as the National Negro Congress, the Southern Negro Youth Congress, and the United Negro and Allied Veterans of World War II.[1]

Yet it was part of Communist propaganda to insist that they *had* penetrated the Association. They had, indeed, lured a few prominent Negroes into their Elysian Fields. Although W.E.B. DuBois, one of NAACP's founders, had for many years resisted their enticements, he had eventually earned at least the label of "fellow-traveler," whereas the glamorous Paul Robeson had gone all the way. The Communists failed to mention that both these men had been repudiated by the NAACP, specifically because of these leanings. But they used them—Robeson especially—to give the impression that infiltration had been successful.

The Communists had still another reason for wanting to prove their success, especially when their failure became apparent to them. This was interesting in view of their pretended friendliness and sympathy toward the oppressed race. By deceiving people generally, not only in the "Black Belt" but throughout the nation, into the belief that there had been a mass migration of Negroes into the Communist camp, they could greatly increase race antagonisms and cause division and chaos—a constant Communist aim. Moreover, in the South, they could spread fear. They allowed it, for example, to leak out that there was a Black Communist plot of insurrection with the intent of founding an independent Negro soviet in the heart of America.[2] Thus

[1] Wilson Record, *The Negro and the Communist Party*, Chapel Hill: University of North Carolina Press, 1951, p. 298.

[2] J. Edgar Hoover, *Masters of Deceit*, p. 244.

they worked on the suspicion which had already been planted in the Congress and in a part of the Southern press until it became panic. This was not the first time the Communists had used frenzied anti-communism as a tool to carve their own ends of division and conquest.

> If [wrote Wilson Record] . . . Negroes refused to be deceived by communist trickery, at least some of the party's "Uncle Toms" could be paraded before the American public in such a way that white supremacists would be convinced of the widespread disloyalty of Negroes in this country.[3]

The "Uncle Toms" were, of course, the few Negroes that had actually joined the Party and were obedient to its commands *even against members of their own race.* This was only one of the demonstrations that Communists cared nothing for the welfare of the Negroes as such. They were interested only in the addition of Negroes to Party or fellow-traveling ranks. This would enlarge the representation in those ranks of the proletariat.

But there were many more such indications. Negroes frequently saw through their deceptions. There was one, for example, who had been invited to attend the Lenin School in Moscow so that he might be trained for propaganda work among members of his race in America. He was young and impressionable, and he accepted the offer believing that "through Communism a better and fairer world could be developed for all mankind." After attending the school for a while, however:

> I found that Negroes were special objects of political exploitation. The sacrifices and dirty work planned for the American Negro Communists as spearheads for communizing the United States made it obvious that we were considered only as pawns in a game where others would get the prize.[4]

[3] Record, *op. cit.*, p. 190.
[4] Hoover, *Masters of Deceit*, p. 250.

3

One day in 1960, Senator Olin Johnston of South Carolina got up in the Senate and made a vehement speech against proposed legislation to introduce federal inspection of election practices in Southern communities, which made it difficult if not impossible for Negroes to vote. He declaimed at length about Communist corruption of the Negro. The Senator would probably have bitterly resented any suggestion that he was a "dupe" of Communist propaganda, yet it was evident that, aided of course by his original prejudice, he had fallen for all the lies that had been told by Party promoters about the success the Communists had had in recruiting Negroes.

Carried away by his conviction that all they declared was true, the Senator made a serious tactical blunder. As support for his contention, he cited a statement made by FBI Director J. Edgar Hoover to the Internal Security Subcommittee in December, 1959. He then asked unanimous consent to spread Hoover's statement upon the *Congressional Record*. When this was granted, he handed the clerk a copy of the statement, but from his subsequent remarks it was apparent that he had digested only part of it. The whole was inserted, however, in the *Record* and there it stands, conspicuously refuting the Senator's claims.

The statement is a description of a convention of the Communist Party U.S.A. Senator Johnston had certainly read as far as this sentence:

> Another of the major aims of the 17th national convention was to reemphasize the recruitment of Negroes into the Communist Party by reembellishing the same old hackneyed phrase alleging that the Communist Party is the savior of the Negro.[5]

This was just what he wanted. Here was the chief of the federal police telling of his certain knowledge of the most vicious Communist propaganda. But did the Senator read the rest of the paragraph?

[5] 106 CR 4106 (Mar. 2, 1960).

It is no secret that one of the bitterest disappointments of communistic efforts in this Nation has been the failure to lure our Negro citizens into the party. Despite every type of propaganda boomed at our Nation's Negro citizens, they have never succumbed to the party's saccharine promises of a Communist Utopia. This generation and generations to come for many years owe a tremendous debt to our Negro citizens who have consistently refused to surrender their freedom for the tyranny of communism.[6]

The Senator seems also to have glanced too hastily at Chapter 18 of Mr. Hoover's book, *Masters of Deceit,* large portions of which he caused to be "spread on the *Record*" in connection with his marathon speech of March 2, 1960. The first excerpt must have been greatly to his liking:

> The Communist Party from its very inception has held itself out as the vanguard of the working class, and as such has sought to assume the role of protector and champion of minorities. It directs special attention, among others, to Negroes and nationality groups.

But how about this, in the same paragraph?

> Actually the vast majority of Negroes and numbers of foreign language groups have rejected communism for what it is—a heartless, totalitarian way of life which completely disregards the dignity of man . . .[7]

It would be too much to expect the busy Senator from South Carolina to have read the following half dozen or so pages from Mr. Hoover's chapter. Nevertheless most of them were put into the *Record* at the Senator's request. For example:

> It becomes obvious that the party, despite great efforts had failed to win over even a significant minority of Negroes . . .

[6] *Ibid.*
[7] 106 CR 4118.

American Negroes had realized that the party was a fraud and a deception and that it was willing to betray the Negro to better serve Soviet Russia . . .

The party has made vigorous attempts to infiltrate the National Association for the Advancement of Colored People (NAACP). The organization in 1950 authorized its board of directors to revoke the charter of any chapter found to be Communist-controlled . . .[8]

Nevertheless, said the Senator:

They filter into organizations such as the NAACP . . .[9]

Later in the same speech, he said:

Mr. President, there is no doubt that the Communist line is to infiltrate our domestic organizations and stir up racial prejudice and violence . . .

The movement for sit-down strikes, coming at the present time when the issue of civil rights, Federal control over voting, is before the Senate, is not a coincidence. The distinguished Senator from Georgia [Mr. Russell] charged that this was an organized sit-down strike movement. I charge further that *this is a communist-inspired and a communist-organized sitdown strike movement.* [Emphasis added.][1]

He added, charitably implying that the Negro participants in the strike were "dupes":

This movement may have been organized innocently, but so far as the Communists are concerned it is now their movement, their front and their project.[2]

Mr. Hoover, however, who seems to have had a higher opin-

[8] *Ibid.*
[9] 106 CR 4106.
[1] *Ibid.* 4120.
[2] *Ibid.*

206

ion of Negro mentality than the Senator, gave chapter and verse to prove that Negroes, especially those who controlled the policies of the NAACP, were anything but gullible.

In 1956, when the NAACP and other organizations sponsored a National Conference on Civil Rights in Washington, the Party attempted to "move in," and started promoting the conference. The NAACP countered by screening the delegates.

Similarly, in 1957, in the Prayer Pilgrimage for Freedom in Washington, the Party again attempted to move in and tried to exploit the pilgrimage as a rallying point for unity. NAACP leaders publicly told the communists that they were not welcome, and steps were taken to keep them off the platform. One outstanding Negro leader even tried to cancel the pilgrimage to prevent communists from propagandizing the event.[3]

Repeatedly, in his book, Mr. Hoover emphasized that the NAACP, which avowedly had helped promote the sit-down strikes that had aroused Senator Johnston's ire, had resisted Communist attempts to "infiltrate" it.

One of the most effective anticommunist measures I have heard of is the following: The NAACP had a meeting in Norfolk, Virginia, presided over by a clergyman. The minister opened the meeting with the simple statement that if any members of the Communist Party were present they would be excused. Silence ensued, with no person leaving. Then the chairman, starting with the front row, asked each individual if he were a communist. All entered denials until he got to the back of the room where the state organizer for the Communist Party was sitting with a white woman. When asked the question, he tried to evade, but the minister pinned him down. The state organizer then stated that he did not think it was proper to ask such a question. The minister calmly replied, "You are excused," and the couple left.[4]

[3] Hoover, *Masters of Deceit*, pp. 246–47.
[4] *Ibid.*, p. 247.

The Hoover chapter continued to give other examples of the Negroes' repudiation of Communist support from Buffalo, San Francisco, Chicago, Detroit, and New York. But the Southern Sixth Column remained unconvinced. Disparagement of the Negro and the organizations that supported him was so important to certain Southern Senators that they were willing to swallow all the Communist propaganda which the Negroes themselves had rejected.

> . . . I doubt seriously [said Senator Strom Thurmond, also of South Carolina] that the NAACP is playing into the hands of the Communists unintentionally.[5]

In support of his doubts, Senator Thurmond spread upon the *Record* a history of the Association in an editorial in the April 18, 1960, issue of the *Sumter Daily Item,* entitled "Information About NAACP the General Public Should Have."[6]

> Attorney-General Eugene Cook of Georgia made an exhaustive study of it and the facts he dug up are startling.
> The record shows that the association originated in New York City 46 years ago as the brain child of a southern scallawag and Russian-trained revolutionary named William E. Walling.

The record also shows that Walling, though he had studied the Russian revolutionary movement of 1905 and had been a socialist, had later repudiated the Bolshevik revolution and had collaborated in the anti-Soviet book *Out of Their Own Mouths.* Also, in 1917, he had "vigorously supported the war and was extremely critical of the Socialist pacifists."[7] These facts Mr. Cook discreetly omitted from his report on his exhaustive study.

In view of the fact that the NAACP was founded, according

---

[5] 106 CR 8362.
[6] *Ibid.*
[7] David Shannon, "William English Walling" in *Dictionary of American Biography,* Supplement Two, p. 290.

to Mr. Cook's own arithmetic, in 1914, when Russia was still under Czarist absolutism and three years before the Bolshevik revolution, the following statement seems somewhat anachronistic:

Mr. Cook says that from the day of its organization "South-hating white people with long records of affinity for affiliating and participation in Communist, Communist front, subversive and fellow traveling organizations, activities, and causes have directed and subsidized the NAACP . . ."[8]

The Attorney General of Georgia then listed officers cited by the House Un-American Activities Committee for affiliation with subversive organizations—citations of the sort we have already seen to be inconclusive of delinquency—and charged that eleven of the twenty-eight NAACP vice-presidents had records of un-American activities (whatever that may mean). Included among these are Oscar Hammerstein II, Bishop W. J. Walls, A. Philip Randolph, and William Lloyd Innes.

Two other vice-presidents and three other directors are well-known apologists for left wing causes. The two vice-presidents are Senator Wayne Morse of Oregon and Eric Johnston of the motion picture industry. The three directors are Mrs. Eleanor Roosevelt, CIO leader Walter Reuther and former Senator Herbert Lehman of New York.

Mr. Cook points out that the racial aims of the Communist Party and those of the NAACP are virtually identical.[9]

4

We have seen some external views of the Negro community and the most significant Negro organization. To complete the picture it might be well to inquire what the Negroes think themselves about the various questions. Perhaps the most thorough investigator of these is Mr. Gunnar Myrdal, whose

[8] 106 CR 8632.
[9] *Ibid.* 8363.

exhaustive book *An American Dilemma* covers the ground up to the year 1944 and does so in a more objective way than most of the writers—Negro and white—who have dealt with the subject.

> To many white people in America, apparently, [writes Mr. Myrdal] it seems natural that they [Negroes] should turn Communist. This is, however, only a testimony of their own bad social conscience and of their ignorance of the Negro community. It is true that a majority of the Negro people are in economic distress. It is also true that they are increasingly becoming conscious of being severely maltreated in America and that they sense social exclusion, which must decrease their feeling of full solidarity with the dominant groups in society. All this should make them open to revolutionary propaganda. It is further true that the Communists have seen their chance and have been devoting much zealous work to cultivating the Negro . . .
>
> Still the Communists have not succeeded in getting any appreciable following among Negroes in America and it does not seem likely that they will . . .
>
> The strong impact of church and religion in the Negro community should not be forgotten. This is, however, only one trait of Negro conservatism. Negroes who care so much for society as to have any general political opinions at all are intent upon "respectability" in a middle class sense. Communism is definitely not respectable in America generally or among Negroes specifically. The unpopularity of Communism in America . . . must, furthermore be uninviting to a group like the American Negroes who know so well that they are unpopular already. As one Negro explained "It is bad enough being black without being black and red."[1]

Mr. Myrdal then quotes the Negro writer James Weldon Johnson:

---

[1] Gunnar Myrdal, *An American Dilemma*, New York: Harper & Brothers, 1944, pp. 508–9.

"In the situation that now exists, it would be positively fool-hardy for us, as a group, to take up the cause of Communistic revolution and thereby bring upon ourselves all the antago-nisms that are directed against it in addition to those we already have to bear . . . ."[2]

But Mr. Myrdal gives still another reason for the repulsion felt by American Negroes for the Russian communism in which the Party has tried to indoctrinate them. With all they have suffered here in their homeland, they are nevertheless Americans and patriotic Americans.

But there is, I am convinced, a still deeper reason why Negroes are so immune against Communism. Negroes are discriminated against in practically all spheres of life, but in their fight for equal opportunity *they have on their side the law of the land and the religion of the nation.* And they know it even down to the poorest stratum. They know that this is their strategic hold. No social Utopia can compete with the American creed which it embodies.[3]

Commenting upon this passage, William A. Nolan in *Communism Versus the Negro* writes:

This has been the most unfavorable situation with which the communists have had to cope. Negroes are Americans and their hopes are rooted in the American way. More recent expressions of the same idea have been made by Negroes themselves. One columnist [Marjorie Mac Kensie in *The Pittsburgh Courier,* April 30, 1949] summed up the Negro mind on America in the following words:

"The Comintern has counted too much on our bitterness and overlooked our faith. It has been too far away to see that we count the prize within our grasp."[4]

[2] James Weldon Johnson, *Negro Americans, What Now?*, New York: The Viking Press, 1934, p. 11. Myrdal, *op. cit.,* p. 509.

[3] Myrdal, *op. cit.,* p. 510.

[4] William A. Nolan, *Communism Versus the Negro,* Chicago: Henry Regnery Co., 1951, p. 22.

211

And in support of the same thesis, Mr. Nolan quotes from the moving keynote address of Roy Wilkins substituting for Walter White at the fortieth annual convention of the NAACP:

> In demanding these things . . . we do not cry out bitterly that we love another land better than our own, or another people better than ours. This is our nation. We helped to build it. . . . We have helped to make it a better land through our songs, our laughter, our expansion and clarification of its Constitution and its Bill of Rights. . . . No, we are Americans, and in the American way, with American weapons, and with American determination to be free, we intend to slug it out, to fight here on this home front if it takes forty more summers—until victory is ours.[5]

5

It is not probable that members of the Southern Sixth Column will soon abandon their precious gimmick linking the hated Negro leaders with the hated Communist Party. Most of these persons in and out of the Congress would generally rather talk than read, and only by reading can they become familiar with the facts. Their way of life and their ways of thought are much like those of the Communists themselves: single-tracked, closed to argument, and with the almost religious devotion to an archaic cause that the Communists maintain toward Marxism.

They are, unwittingly, one of communism's most effective allies. Despite the Communists' greatest failure, the Southern Sixth Column accords them full success. In their effort to turn Americans against an exceedingly large racial minority among their fellow-citizens they are relieving the Communists of much of their labor in dividing the Nation and thus preparing, as they think, for its defeat.

Fortunately in the very heart of the South, even of the Deep South, the Column is being bravely combated. Men, women, newspapers, and books circulate in every state, proclaiming

[5] *The Crisis*, August, 1949, p. 262. Nolan, *op. cit.*, pp. 22–23.

that political equality unlimited by factors of race and color is a right unalienable from an American citizen. On social or economic equality they may disagree: these are not necessarily conceded even by those who are convinced that Negroes are American citizens. On such questions the horizon has not yet cleared. But as long as persons born and bred in the Southland know that the United States is truly a democracy and therefore immune to any totalitarian doctrine, they strengthen the nation far more than any parochial fight against a Communist chimera can ever do. And such Southerners bulk large.

XIV.   Subversion by the Far Right

MANY AMERICANS have felt that, except for the Communist Party U.S.A., the nearest thing to a Communist organization in America is the John Birch Society. Representatives of the Catholic Church, of several Protestant sects, of the American Jewish Congress, editorials in many of the nation's newspapers, college professors, and scientists have pointed out that both in structure and procedure the Society follows the Communist pattern almost exactly. In behavior, these observers say, its supporters have imitated the subversive conduct of radical extremists, even to the planting and detonation of bombs. Although there is, as yet, no evidence that it advocates the overthrow of the United States government by force and violence, its leaders have attacked fundamentals of the American faith—such as, for example, belief in democracy. It promotes the bankruptcy of the government by advocating abolition of the income tax.

Why, under these circumstances, it has not been investigated by the House Committee on Un-American Activities seems a logical question. Yet to those who have studied the history of that committee, its reluctance to disparage any group that calls itself "anti-Communist," however un-American it may be in other directions, is understandable.

The John Birch Society does indeed profess anti-communism, though that profession is debatable. That it has helped the Communist cause has been stated in the Russian press.[1] It has accused a Republican President and his Secretary of State of

[1] See pp. 93–94 *supra*.

treason. It has adopted the devices of a secret society so that its true intentions have been veiled. If, indeed, the John Birch Society were organized in Moscow and maintained by Russian support and funds, this would well accord with some of its chief's own indiscreet pronouncements.

This chief, the society's founder, Robert Welch, has stated a principle of "reversal" in his analysis of Communist propaganda. Communists, he thinks, will announce that they favor something in order that Americans may be against it. Contrariwise, they may inveigh against some view or movement so that we may favor it. He suggests, therefore, that the Russians may organize groups which *pretend* to be fighting communism but are really supporting it.

Some of them [Mr. Welch concedes] have no more harmful purpose than merely to drain off, into innocuous wastefulness, money and effort which might otherwise find its way into really patriotic and anti-Communist activities. Others are primarily designed to offer protective coloration to Communists who can thus get themselves publicized as active in anti-Communist organizations.[2]

Such a suggestion might well become the basis for hearings by the House Un-American Activities Committee on whether the John Birch Society is what it pretends to be.

Art Buchwald, who under a humorous cover often makes penetrating and profound observations, once wrote a column for the *New York Herald Tribune* entitled "The Orlov Plan."[3] His story was that he had met a Russian comrade named Serge Orlov at Maxim's in Paris. To the genial accompaniment of vodka, they became friendly and his acquaintance spoke of the Orlov Plan and asked Buchwald if he had heard of it. When Buchwald said no, Orlov explained that it had been so successful

[2] Robert Welch, *Blue Book of the John Birch Society*, published by the Society 1958, p. 160.
[3] Dec. 12, 1961.

215

that he had been decorated for it by the Soviet government and he had been put in charge of all internal subversion in the United States.

For years the Soviets had tried to infiltrate labor unions and liberal groups without success. But, Orlov suggested, how about working through the Right Wing—the so-called anti-Communists? The extremists in this camp were the only Americans really willing to wreck their government. So Orlov proposed to get the Right Wingers to accuse Eisenhower of being a Communist and government officials of treason, to attack the U.N., to spread conflict between army officers and civilians, and to oppose education and health measures. Finally, anyone who disagreed with all this was to be called a Communist.

Orlov said that when he first told of his plan in Moscow, people in the Kremlin thought he was crazy, but, as they had nothing to lose, they told him to go ahead. Buchwald, he said, could see for himself how successful he had been. Americans themselves had sown the seeds of doubt about America. Now the Russians could sit back and watch their work being done for them.

This is one of the most penetrating of all Buchwald's satirical essays. If it were literally factual instead of being fictionally presented truth, the results would have been the same. Nothing could have been more to the liking of the Soviets than these efforts by Americans to "wreck their government"—not by force and violence, but by more insidious and subtle means.

2

When Mr. Welch first came out with his sensational and provocative pronouncements, the temptation to ridicule the whole movement became irresistible, and columnists, editorial writers, and cartoonists in every part of the country did not resist it. The apparently pathological motivations of its leading supporters hardly seemed to deserve serious comment. To some observers, the Society seemed only another of the irrelevant aberrations that were common in the lunatic fringe during the 1920's—the flagpole sittings, for example, or the marathon dances. But to others, the John Birch Society was not a wholly irrelevant phenomenon.

There was, for instance, a connection between it and the McCarthyism which attracted such a swarm of supposedly intelligent Americans in the 1950's. Along the road to the John Birch fantastic summit were all the "patriotic" groups we have observed: the American Legion, the Veterans of Foreign Wars, the Daughters of the American Revolution, and lesser clusters of flag-wavers. It carried the practices of the House Committee on Un-American Activities, the Senate Internal Security Sub-committee, certain loyalty boards, and certain Attorneys General to their ultimate and insane conclusion. It gave the impression, therefore, of being related to the whole of the American anti-Communist movement.

Those who had lived through the hysteria that followed the first World War, those who had seen the similar though more controlled panic after the war of the 1940's, could not altogether laugh off the John Birch Society. Insignificant as were the statistics of its membership, it showed familiar symptoms. It was, for example, strongly isolationist, insisting that the danger was internal. It advocated the suppression of free speech. It opposed labor organization. But most important of all, it was seen at the crest of a wave: a wave of "conservatism." Below it, but only just below, were somewhat more rational insurgencies: the Newburgh plan for reducing welfare activities, the Barry Goldwater-for-President campaign conducted by remnants of the Taft Republicans, and countless smaller Rightist clubs and leagues. Some appeared on college campuses: to the surprise of many of us, boys and girls tagged themselves as "conservatives." (If we could recapture some of the basic meanings with which English words started, we would call such groups "radical" for they were composed of rebels against the norm rather than its conservators.)

Thus, more and more Americans of the old school—those who cherished traditional American values—took the John Birch Society and its abundant spawn seriously. They realized that, following the Communist line, it had established "fronts" with innocent names covering wide territory. And they knew that however unsound the look of Birchism, it had had its way carefully paved for it over as many years as communism itself had endured.

Taking the Birch Society seriously had one effect that encouraged opponents of the Sixth Column. Its paradoxical aims were given wide publicity. This recruited many opponents and "Birchism" became unpopular. It had the effect, then, of splitting the Sixth Column. "Lesser breeds" such as the *National Review* did not want to be associated with it. Senator Goldwater repudiated any suggestion that he was a "Bircher." If these dissensions continued, it was hoped that the Sixth Column might topple from the weight that Robert Welch had put upon it.

Serious discussion of the John Birch Society is having another effect. Americans are beginning to wonder if, perhaps, there is something unsound in the whole isolated practice of anti-communism in the United States. We are wondering, for example, if indeed the problem is an internal one at all; if, perhaps, the parochial view is one that the Russians want us to take because it will divert our eyes from the realities in Moscow, in Prague, in Cracow, and in Budapest.

3

One of the most cogent protests against Robert Welch's apparently subversive organization came in the state of California —territory in which he had hoped to secure a host of followers. No federal agency of justice, no federal attorney general has yet undertaken an investigation of the John Birch Society. But the Department of Justice of the state of California has done just that. Its Attorney General, Stanley Mosk, and his assistant Howard Jewel made a careful analysis of the Society and, in July, 1961, sent a report thereon to Governor Edmund G. Brown.

The report is a masterpiece of clarity and vigor. Its occasional satirical and even humorous expression does not detract from the seriousness with which these officials regard their subject. Nor do they hesitate to suggest that though the Society at first provided a field day for the journalistic wags, the time for ridicule is past.

The cadre of the John Birch Society [reads the preamble to the report] seems to be formed primarily of wealthy businessmen, retired military officers and little old ladies in tennis shoes. They are bound together by an obsessive fear of "communism," a word which they define to include any ideas differing from their own, even though these ideas may differ even more markedly with the ideals of Marx, Engels, Lenin, and Khrushchev. In response to this fear they are willing to give up a large measure of the freedoms guaranteed them by the United States Constitution in favor of accepting the dictates of their "Founder."[4]

The report explains that the "Founder" who insists on the use of that title—always, written with a capital *F*—is "an embittered candy maker of Belmont, Massachusetts, and a former member of the Board of Directors of the National Association of Manufacturers." It quotes Mr. Welch as saying, "The John Birch Society will operate under completely authoritative control at all levels." It shows from the Founder's own words that disloyalty or dissent in the ranks will not be tolerated. Any difference of opinion will be eliminated "without going through any congress or so-called democratic processes." It recounts instances of the Founder's refusal to hold press conferences or to answer the questions of members of the press or television corps. These regulations are all quoted from the *Blue Book of The John Birch Society*, published in 1958.

In six ways, the report continues, the John Birch Society is similar to the Communist Party.

1. Standard Communist strategy for countries marked for take-over is to sow in those countries seeds of doubt and sus-

[4] Report of Attorney General Stanley Mosk of California to Governor Edmund G. Brown, July 7, 1961. (hereafter designated as "Report."), p. 1.

picion against the government and leaders. Here the John Birch Society "Founder" has accused a former President of the United States, a former Secretary of State, the Chief Justice of the United States, the Chief of CIA and other top-ranking government leaders with treason. Thus does the John Birch Society do the work of Communists.

2. The John Birch Society is implacably opposed to the most effective of the free world's defenses against Communism. [Marshall Plan, U.N., Nato, defense spending]. Their opposition against these defenses is matched only by that of Khrushchev and Mao Tse-tung.

3. Domestically, the John Birch Society opposes civil rights, collective bargaining, and the social gospel of religions.

4. The Birch Society believes in the organization of "fronts." "We would organize fronts—little fronts, big fronts, temporary fronts, permanent fronts, all kinds of fronts." [Quote from *Blue Book*, page 86.]

5. One of the least appealing of Welch's teachings is his open espousal of techniques which he himself terms "mean and dirty" . . . These tactics include the disruption of peaceful public meetings. [The report gives case histories.]

6. The Birch Society is a monolithic authoritarian organization with the policy dictated from above and no dissent permitted in its ranks. [Exactly so, says the report, is the Communist Party.][5]

This fifteen-page report was sent to the Governor July 7, 1961. It was widely quoted in the Nation's press, including the *New York Times* which published an article by the report's authors on August 20, 1961.

4

The Birch Society and other groups of what Alan Barth has called "The Rampageous Right"[6]—many of which are disguised

[5] Report, pp. 7–10.
[6] Alan Barth, "Report on the 'Rampageous Right'" in *New York Times Magazine*, Nov. 24, 1961.

"fronts" regimented under Welch control—have been attacked on so many sides that their critics hope for public reappraisal of the whole current anti-Communist movement in America. Unless the pendulum of opinion swings too far, there may result a realistic anti-Communist force which will oppose Communism in the American way leading not from weakness but from strength.

Especially eloquent against the extremists of the right have been American religious groups. When Mr. Welch made the charge that seven thousand Protestant ministers in the United States "can fairly be called Communists or Communist sympathizers," 137 Southern California ministers issued a statement calling Welch's statement a vicious attack, adding:

Any group or individual, however well intentioned, that promotes a program of hatred, suspicion and distrust of our free American institutions . . . is unwittingly serving the cause of those who would destroy those institutions.[7]

Probably nowhere in the world is there so consistent and determined a voice against communism as in the Roman Catholic Church. For this very reason, American Catholics are coming to deplore the methods of the far Right which, as the Reverend Father John F. Cronin maintains, are aiding rather than obstructing the propagandist efforts of the Communist Party. These opinions are emphatically stated in a booklet by this priest entitled *Communism: Threat to Freedom,* published in March, 1962, by the National Catholic Welfare Conference. Excerpts from the booklet were part of a news story in the *New York Times.*[8]

In many parts of the country, [writes the Reverend Father Cronin] hysteria and suspicion are becoming increasingly evident. A virulent form of disunity is weakening us in the world struggle against communism and performing this dis-

[7] Report (California), p. 3.
[8] Mar. 2, 1962.

service in the name of militant anticommunism. Many Americans are confused and bewildered by the whole trend . . .

He draws special attention to the obsession that has been at the heart of nearly all the American militant movements that communism is a domestic problem. In the John Birch Society this obsession has crystallized into a basic doctrine. Father Cronin says:

> Those who would have Americans concentrate on a minor threat of domestic subversion and ignore subversion and Communist pressures in Europe, Asia, Africa, and Latin America are misleading the American people. Whatever their motives, they are effectively aiding the Communist cause.

After many examples of fallacious arguments put forth by right-wing groups, such as insistence on the successful subversion of Negroes by Communist agents, subversion of the Protestant clergy and in the Jewish community, Father Cronin gives some positive advice to sincere anti-Communists:

> For the average citizen who asks: What can I do to fight communism? the answer might well be: Devote all your strength and energy in concert with your fellow Americans, to build national unity and moral strength . . . Even in dealing with moral evils, concentrate less on denunciation and more on giving leadership and example . . . Do your part to make this a better and stronger nation, and we shall not fear what the Communists plot and scheme against us.

A recent report entitled "The Radical Right: A Fact Sheet" was prepared by the Commission on Law and Social Action of the American Jewish Congress.

> The extreme right movement [believes the Commission] draws its strength from American frustration. Those who accept its fantasies do so in flight from their unwillingness to accept the imperfections of the world they live in. One of those

imperfections is the fact that America is in a cold war in which it must occasionally take some defeats.

After ten pages of exposure of fallacies in the programs of the John Birch Society, of Dr. Fred C. Schwarz's "Christian Anti-Communist Crusade," of Hargis's "Christian Crusade," of Dr. George S. Benson's "National Education Program," and of "Young Americans for Freedom," the "Fact Sheet" quotes a resolution adopted by the American Jewish Congress in 1961—a resolution aimed primarily at the John Birch Society but applicable to other right-wing groups:

> There must be effective opposition in order to assure that the aims of the Society will be defeated. We must strive to make clear to all Americans that it would be a tragedy for our country and the world if the program of the John Birch Society were to prevail. We should also expose the fact that its appeal to super-patriotism is a device to stampede the American people into abandoning many hard-won victories in the struggle against poverty and insecurity.

5

Some time in 1957, a number of Harvard graduates formed a committee for the actual though unavowed purpose of destroying their alma mater. (This, at least, is the belief of other Harvard alumni.) With an unawareness of irony characteristic of persons on their level of intelligence they named the committee "Veritas." A year later, the committee, having secured the funds always available to rightist groups, became the "Veritas Foundation." The foundation stated as its objective:

> To educate the officials, teaching staffs, governing bodies, undergraduates and graduates of American colleges and universities upon the subject of communism, the international communist conspiracy and its methods of infiltration into the United States.[9]

[9] Letter from Veritas Foundation Trustees to Harvard graduates, Sept., 1961.

223

The three trustees of the foundation were not precisely educators. One was in the insurance business, two others in the banking or brokerage businesses. All were graduates of Harvard; none had aspired during his formal education to any degree higher than A.B. or S.B. The foundation which was entrusted to these persons undertook to re-educate those who had attended or were professors of American institutions of learning, including their own, then in its fourth century of existence.

The original grievance against Harvard which this group held was the university's invitation to Dr. J. Robert Oppenheimer to become a William James Lecturer on Philosophy and Psychology. In 1954, Dr. Oppenheimer had been found by a majority opinion of the Atomic Energy Commission "not entitled to the continued confidence of the Government and of this Commission because of the proof of fundamental defects in his character." Later, however, a special panel of the AEC Personnel Security Board headed by Gordon Gray came to a "clear conclusion which should be reassuring to the people of this country that he is a loyal citizen."

It is hardly necessary to defend this great scientist, who has made such significant contributions to the American defense effort, against such baseless charges. His has been a *cause célèbre* and he has been abundantly vindicated. In any case the relevance of his security status to his Harvard lectures was not clear except to the Veritas Committee and its disciples.

> In making the appointment [stated the University Corporation] Harvard was conscious that its act might be construed as an effort to challenge the Government's position and as a gesture of sympathy to Dr. Oppenheimer. If this had been Harvard's purpose it would indeed deserve criticism. But such was not the case. The choice was based entirely on the positive qualities of Dr. Oppenheimer.

Harvard has always tried to arrive at sound conclusions despite the possibility of controversy over them. In this connection it may be pertinent to recall the words of William James on this subject:

"The university most worthy of rational admiration is that

224

one in which your lonely thinker can feel himself least lonely, most positively furthered . . . The day when Harvard shall stamp a single hard and fast type of character upon her children will be that of her downfall. Our undisciplinables are our proudest product. Let us agree that the output of them will never cease."[1]

The Veritas Foundation, established in July, 1958, owing a certain debt to citizens who were worried about their security once the Communists take over and feared lest they be hanged for their wealth to lampposts in the public squares, naturally turned its attention toward Harvard's economics department. It discovered, there, a horrid situation. Professors were expounding the new economic theories of a twentieth-century economist, John Maynard Keynes, who had revealed weaknesses in the postulates of Adam Smith laid down at the beginning of the first industrial revolution. Smith had later been canonized in America as champion of the legendary free enterprise which nostalgic American businessmen still, in 1958, equated with the goddess of liberty, the screaming eagle, and the American flag.

The economic experts in Veritas decided, therefore, to put a stop to the teaching of Keynesian economics at Harvard. They prepared a booklet of 114 pages entitled *Keynes at Harvard,* showing that the British economist and his disciples were Communists or fellow-travelers, and sent it with a covering letter to a list of Harvard graduates.

Dear Harvard Alumnus [read the letter]: Are you disturbed at the evidence of Harvard's trend to the left? Do you realize that socialism prepares the ground for communism? . . .

Won't you help us combat the Fabian-Marxist-Communist front by aiding sound American education before it is too late. Please send checks to Veritas Foundation.

As a result of this campaign, the University and its President, Dr. Nathan Pusey, received an avalanche of letters.

[1] Harvard University Corporation, "A Background Memorandum on the Appointment of Dr. Robert Oppenheimer," pp. 3–4.

I must say [wrote a Ph.D. alumnus] that I do not feel the Veritas group is deliberately trying to promote Communist Party membership, though they practically invite the Harvard Economics Department to fill out Party cards. The group evidently feels that the free enterprise system is in dire peril, so much so that they feel impelled to denounce the free results of academic freedom which they profess to uphold. If free enterprise is so weak, however, as to lie helpless before the onslaught of the Harvard Keynesians, perhaps it does need after all to be analyzed in terms other than the glorious mythology of supply and demand curves that pleases the Veritas people . . . It is distressing to see Harvard's motto abused in the service of such fear-ridden obscurantism.

Another holder of two degrees wrote:

I fear subversion of our American democratic ideals by Harvard alumni in the Veritas Foundation as much as I do by communist agents.

A lawyer wrote:

Like most of those who speak the viewpoint which the Veritas Foundation presents, these self-styled conservatives are in effect anarchists who, if their program succeeded, would bring social order into ruin by their negativism.

Another lawyer stated that:

Veritas Foundation works to subvert the order it purports to protect, by sowing distrust of good faith where mature men would be willing to debate differences within a framework of realistic trust.

It would be unavailing further to pursue the subject of the Veritas Foundation. Harvard will doubtless survive its attacks and will preserve its academic freedom as it has always done "through change and through storm." It is wise to know, how-

226

ever, of the existence of this particular brand of subversion in the interest of which men will turn upon an institution they once loved and hit it below the waist.

6

"Book-burning" is not a new American exercise. Leagues and societies which thought they were protecting the morals of the young have often tried to prohibit the sale or mailing of literature which they pronounced "obscene," "pornographic," or "lewd." The late Anthony Comstock, founder of the New York Society for the Suppression of Vice, and his successor, John S. Sumner, were notorious book-burners, and so were their counterparts in the Boston Watch and Ward Society. In the nineteenth century, what was known as "comstockery" included many books of all kinds in its attacks on every form of artistic expression.

Of late years, these book-burners have been joined by members of rightist fronts who have tried to exclude books from schools and libraries because they were "subversive." Books were pronounced objectionable on this ground if they appeared sympathetic to socialism or communism or even if they merely explained these philosophies; if they were critical of free enterprise or of certain events in American history such as the Mexican war; if they endorsed the Democratic party, Franklin Roosevelt, or the New Deal; or (in the South) racial integration. All such books were believed by extremists of the Right to be unfit for young and impressionable minds.

The combination of such book-burners with the traditional burners of "indecent" books produced some confusion. For example, there were repeated attempts to ban *1984* by George Orwell. This is, of course, one of the bitterest attacks on communism ever written. It contains, however, certain passages thought by prurient critics to be obscene. (Any passage which refers to entirely normal sex relations between a man and a woman is pronounced "obscene.")

Thus, in Wrenshall, Minnesota, the high school English

227

teacher Richard C. Wyman received a letter from school super-
intendent E. C. Hedegard stating:

> This book, *1984*, is not part of our English program and is out-
> lawed from use in our public school and the library copy will
> be withdrawn immediately. Any book or article which deals
> with sex openly or by inference, whether on the approved
> library list or not, will not be used in this school and students
> shall not be encouraged to read it.[2]

Mr. Wyman, who had asked the students in his advanced-
section twelfth-year English class to read and report on the book,
had evidently read it with such concentration on its anti-Communist appeal that he had ignored the passages on sex.

He was ordered to withdraw his assignment. He refused and
was fired by the school board which had unanimously decided
that the book was "immoral and obscene." Fortunately the Minnesota Civil Liberties Union went to Wyman's defense. And an
editorial in the *Minneapolis Tribune* stated:

> Obviously, had Wyman obeyed the board, he would have
> destroyed his usefulness as a teacher in the eyes of his pupils.
> They never again would have been able to rely on an assign-
> ment given them. The teacher's integrity as a professional per-
> son was at stake here.[3]

As a result of a petition signed by a hundred Wrenshall citizens, Wyman was reinstated, but only on condition that he should
use *1984* on an "optional" basis.[4]

Orwell's book was also adversely scrutinized in Texas along
with Steinbeck's *The Grapes of Wrath,* Thomas Wolfe's *Of Time
and the River,* and *Brave New World* by Aldous Huxley. A member of the John Birch Society in Texas also objected to *Living*

[2] American Book Publishers Council, Inc., *Freedom to Read Bulletin,*
March, 1962, pp. 7–8.
[3] Oct. 25, 1961.
[4] *Freedom to Read Bulletin,* p. 8.

228

Biographies of Great Philosophers by Henry and Dana Lee Thomas because of Plato's advocacy of communal living. "I can't help but believe," said this Bircher, "that this is one reason we have so many sex maniacs walking around." The notion that persons are driven to sex mania by the perusal of Plato's *Republic* is a novel one indeed.[5]

On the racial issue, *Rabbit's Wedding* by Garth Williams was attacked on the ground that a union of a white rabbit with a black one was miscegenation. J. Everett Haley, leader of the rightist group Texans for America, fought against textbooks that showed both sides of a controversy. "Until children are old enough," Haley said, "to understand both sides of a question, they should be taught only the American side."[6]

In California, a fifth grade student was told by his teacher to take home a copy of *The Wonderful Wizard of Oz* by L. Frank Baum because the author was suspected of having Communist sympathies. In Meriden, Connecticut, a group calling themselves "ultra-conservatives" and as members of the Daughters of the American Revolution or the Citizens Anti-Communist Committee of Connecticut, condemned fourteen out of sixteen social studies books used in the local school system because they were "soft on Communism" or "favored the U.N., federal aid and world government." The attack named authors Pearl Buck, Henry Steele Commager, Norman Cousins, Oliver LaFarge, Lincoln Steffens, Dorothy Canfield Fisher, David S. Muzzey, and Stuart Chase.[7]

Fortunately, the American Book Publishers Council has been able to report that in nearly every case it has cited, there has been stern protest against attempted book banning by local citizens, local newspapers, and state boards of education. Here, then, is another case in which those on the far Right have reduced their cause to absurdity.

[5] *Ibid.*, p. 10.
[6] *Ibid.*, p. 10.
[7] *Ibid.*, p. 5.

7

A late echo of the voice of Senator Joseph McCarthy was heard on April 5, 1962, in the testimony of former Major General Edwin A. Walker before the Special Senate Preparedness Subcommittee. Walker had been rebuked for his indoctrination of troops on political matters and had resigned from the army so that he might present his case to the American people.

Walker described himself as the "scapegoat" of what he supposed was the United States government's deliberate collaboration with communism. He placed the responsibility for this on the shoulders of Secretary of State Dean Rusk and Walt Whitman Rostow, head of the State Department's Policy Planning Council. He further supported the John Birch Society's contention that former President Eisenhower was "soft on communism," an accusation which he also applied to President Kennedy. By this policy, Walker said, the United States was "digging its own grave for Khrushchev to bury us in" and that the grave was "three feet deep" already. There is, he said, a "hidden control apparatus" which is dictating a "no-win" policy toward the world Communist conspiracy. Both Rusk and Rostow, he maintained, were "very influential" in this apparatus.

As a climax to his testimony in the two-day hearing, Walker made a physical attack on a reporter who asked him an embarrassing question.

The difference between Walker and McCarthy is that Walker appears to be entirely sincere in his beliefs. It is unlikely that he has anything to gain by his fantastic testimony. As the *New York Times* has pointed out "there is no reason to question his good faith."[8]

For Mr. Walker [says the *Times*] lives in a conspiratorial dream world, and in such a world conspirators abound.

The *Times* adds what may be taken as a word of warning lest we dismiss him as an isolated crackpot.

[8] *New York Times,* Apr. 6, 1962.

230

Mr. Walker is not the only dweller in that world. He has many others with him. For most of them, when things go wrong, "conspiracy" is the answer. Has Russia got the atomic bomb? Do the Communists rule continental China? Is there trouble in the Congo? Why did we stop short of the 38th parallel in Korea? Was this "no-win" policy the work of traitors? Are we drifting toward the welfare state? Any other worries? Plainly, somebody is plotting things.[9]

It is possible that Walker's outburst has been more damaging to the John Birch, rightist cause than anything that has been said or done. Yet we are living in a time when hysteria, as it has been before, may be just around the corner.

[9] *Ibid.*

231

XV.   Conclusions

THAT ANTI-COMMUNISM in the United States has been consistently hampered by panic is the wholly logical effect of a cause. To appreciate it one must examine the basic aim of communism as expounded by Karl Marx and interpreted—though he did not always follow it—by Lenin. The original concept was one that the American mind cannot easily grasp, and it is human nature to fear what one does not comprehend. Furthermore, as we have seen, it has been the purpose of certain American demagogues to exploit that fear by exaggerating the issue the Marxist doctrine presents or by beclouding it, in order to increase their own political power.

Americans in general have never been afraid of war. American soldiers marched without fear into the known and understood combat with other soldiers in 1918 and armies, navies, air forces, and people united in courage when, in the 1940's, huge pressures on two fronts opposed them.

But the Russian menace is different from any we have faced. The cold war seems to bear no resemblance to the shooting wars of the past. In it, armies and navies play no apparent part. The arms race may continue but it seems to lead nowhere, even if we won it, even if we moved far ahead of the Russians, the strange, veiled threat would still be there. For communism is a phantom thing; it moves its cold ghostly fingers among us, it is eternally elusive; it is under the bed, in the closet, in the house, perhaps, of our next-door neighbor; it wields a subtle, mysteri-

232

ous weapon unlike a knife or a gun or even a hundred megaton bomb.

No one has made this as clear as George Kennan, who has spent most of a lifetime studying Russian history, language, philosophy, politics, and social conditions. He has had difficulty, he says, explaining this "simple fact," as he calls it, to Americans, yet most of us have known of its existence. What Mr. Kennan has found hard to explain, perhaps, is that the Russian goal has been and will continue to be largely unattainable and that once we look the thing squarely in the face, it will cease to scare us.

The Marxist-Leninist ideology [he said in one of his lectures to university students] did not suggest that it was by a single grand military conflict between the world of Communism and the world of capitalism that these aims were to be achieved. I cannot think of a time when the Soviet government desired that there should be such a conflict, planned to launch it, or staked its hopes and expectations for the victory of world socialism on the effects of such an encounter. Central to the Soviet view of how socialism was to triumph on a world scale has always been the operation of social and political forces within the capitalist countries; and while Moscow has always recognized that civil violence would have a legitimate place in the operation of these processes—while it has not hesitated in certain instances to promote or even to organize such civil violence; while it has even considered, in fact, that the use of the Soviet armies in a subsidiary capacity might be justified at one point or another as a means of hastening or completing an otherwise inevitable process—it has never regarded action by its own forces as the *main* agency for the spread of world revolution. It has not, in other words, sought to obtain its objectives by the traditional processes of open and outright warfare.[1]

[1] George F. Kennan, *Russia and the West under Lenin and Stalin*, Boston: Little, Brown and Co., 1961, p. 389.

Here, then, is the perfect formula for the practice of the demagogue. He can use it in whatever distorted form pleases him to spread fear not of Russia but of ourselves, to pit one American against another American, to make each citizen suspicious of his neighbor, to foment what Telford Taylor has called a "cold civil war" and thus gain for himself the sort of political power that derives from potential blackmail. He can expose, he says, the Communists that are hiding everywhere among us—meaning those who may dare vote against him. To those who will vote for him, however, he can promise a tough fight against revolution.

The resulting scare has greatly encouraged the Communists who have pursued the Marxist-Leninist aims. It has weakened the faith of the American people in their democracy—the only defense we have against class conflict. It has convinced the men of property that the democratic practices which have insured our survival for nearly two centuries are useless in thwarting the revolutionary impulses of the workers; that only authoritarian tactics—the Communist techniques—are effective against the Communist conspiracy.

The acute fear that afflicted a very considerable portion of the American people when the Soviet doctrine of world revolution was first presented to them became, in time, a chronic fear. As such, it endured beyond the point at which the threat had changed its nature. The Sixth Column kept it alive. This is one of the reasons why, as Kennan says, "American opinion has often been something more than a decade behind the times." With the second World War bringing to the Russians territorial gains in capitalist countries that were *not* the result of proletarian revolution, other factors entered the thinking of the Party's top brass —notably that of Josef Stalin. The Soviets had found another form of conquest that was more sure and less complex than that of internal revolution. Though they established pro-Communist puppet régimes in Czechoslovakia, Poland, Hungary, and East Germany, they acquired and held these so-called satellites by armed force or the threat of armed force, not through popular internal rebellion. And surely, for example, the taking over of the Baltic nations was not because the Latvians, the Esthonians, and the Lithuanians willed it.

In Britain and the United States, moreover, Russian Communists had little success in winning over the huge industrial proletariats of these traditionally capitalist countries. In the United States, especially, trade unions had become so powerful—though there was undoubtedly Communist influence here and there among the organizations—that they were in no mood to subordinate their power to a political dictatorship. In general, American workers were well aware that American prosperity had come through capitalistic enterprise and being prosperous themselves beyond any earlier proletarian dreams they had little wish for a change of economies. Thus, even in the depressed 1930's, but certainly later, the Russians had little more success than the agents of Marx and Engels had had in the 1850's on the heels of the *Communist Manifesto.* Yet as the menace drew further and further away, the fear of it, in the United States, increased. This curious paradox prompted Kennan to say,

> . . . when, in the late 1940's, numbers of worthy people in this country suddenly and belatedly discovered the rather normal phenomenon of foreign penetration and espionage, and set out frantically trying to persuade us that *we* ought to lose faith in *ourselves* because *they* had made this discovery, the evil of Communist subversion over which they were so excited was one which had actually reached its highest point several years earlier and was by that time definitely on the wane. [Italics in original.][2]

Even under normal circumstances American public opinion, especially that dominated by right-wing or Tory influence, is reluctant to change. With the constant chimeras and alarms of the Sixth Column, however, it is virtually impossible for it to do so.

[2] *Ibid.,* p. 397.

235

Today, [added Kennan, supporting his theory that American public opinion lags behind events] there are many equally worthy people who appear to be discovering for the first time that there was such a thing as the Stalin era, and who evidently have much difficulty in distinguishing it from what we have known since 1953. I could even name professional "sovietologists," private and governmental, who seem afraid to admit to themselves or to others that Stalin is really dead.[3]

2

Those who watch the United States from afar are likely to exaggerate American tendencies and trends. Englishmen and continental Europeans as well often mistake the vocal America for the real America—though, as Stephen Vincent Benét pointed out in his epic, *John Brown's Body*, the "real America" is more difficult to see than in earlier days.

There was, however, an article in the *London Observer* about the Cuban invasion, which, though it may be guilty of over-generalization, contains suggestions for a more balanced view than that of our fear-ridden citizens.

To a far greater extent [the *Observer* states] than they would like to admit, our American friends are prisoners of an ideology almost as narrow as that of the Communists and just as fervently believed. The American ideology equates capitalism not only with freedom but very nearly with virtue . . .

To nearly all Americans, Communism is an evil as absolute as Nazism or murder, and any one who questions this dogma must already be infected by the contagion. They decline to notice any difference between Khrushchev's Russia and Stalin's Russia. They ignore the case of Yugoslavia, where Communists have created a society that is independent of Russia and which appears to less impassioned democrats morally no worse than the capitalistic societies of Franco's Spain, Salazar's Portugal, or Verwoerd's South Africa.[4]

[3] *Ibid.*
[4] Reprinted in *New York Herald Tribune*, May 12, 1961, editorial page.

While it is happily untrue that "nearly all Americans" are as obsessed with these convictions as the *Observer's* writer supposes, it is incontrovertible that it is an American tendency to see only the blacks and the whites; to be blind to the nuances. From the practical standpoint, it is extremely unfortunate that so many believe that a Communist is an incarnation of Satan whether he be a Russian, a Yugoslav, a Chinese, or an Albanian. To a practical student of international politics a solution is often reached by "knocking their heads together." If we can manage to pit one camp of Communists against each other, we may liquidate the menace of a united front opposed to us. That is the strategy used by the Communists among our allies. It is the strategy of all psychological warfare. Our separation, for example, of the Italians from the Germans in the late war was a factor of victory.

But to American zealots, the support of any nation which embraces communism is immoral. Like many issues which other nations face as facts or conditions, the Communist issue is to us wholly a moral one. A Communist is not merely a political or economic adversary; he is antichrist. Unless we fight him tooth-and-nail regardless of his nationality or brand of communism, Heaven will be denied us. We must hate him; on our knees before the Almighty, we must hate him.

Thus our administrations—both Democratic and Republican —have been rebuked for lending money and giving assistance to Yugoslavia whose leader and people have sometimes felt the Russian menace as we have.

Another tendency not only of the Sixth Column but of many of its innocent followers is to draw no distinction between Communists and their Socialist enemies. There is confusion, too, about the ideologies of socialism and communism. It is also part of the dogma that degrees of socialization cannot exist. Yet it is obvious that socialized medicine in England has not turned the nation into a socialized (or communized) state. The United States remains defiantly capitalistic in spite of social security, federal aid to schools and colleges, and the wholly nationalized postal service.

237

If, as we have seen has happened before, the pendulum again comes to rest midway between the extremes of the giant swings, we cannot afford complacency. In any interval in which the Sixth Column seems to be marking time we must build roadblocks along its future line of march. And the material of those roadblocks must be that which has built our nation from its beginning: faith in democracy with equal justice for all and a government of laws, not of men.

Bibliography

BOOKS, ARTICLES, ETC.

Angell, Ernest, "The Legion's Betrayal" in *The Nation*, May 24, 1933.

Baker, Roscoe, *The American Legion and American Foreign Policy*. New York: Bookman Associates, 1954.

Barck, Oscar Theodore, Jr., and Nelson Manfred Blake, *Since 1900: A History of the United States in Our Times*. New York: The Macmillan Co., 1947.

Barth, Alan, *Government by Investigation*. New York: The Viking Press, 1955.

———, *The Loyalty of Free Men*. New York: The Viking Press, 1951.

———, "Report on the Rampageous Right" in *The New York Times Magazine*, Nov. 24, 1961.

Bass, Cyrus, *Joe McCarthy, Apostle of Communism*. Chicago: Atomic Age Publishers, 1954.

Bentley, Elizabeth, *Out of Bondage*. New York: Devin-Adair Co., 1951.

Biddle, Francis, *The Fear of Freedom*, Introduction by Harold L. Ickes. Garden City, N.Y.: Doubleday & Co., Inc., 1951.

Buckley, William F., Jr., and L. Brent Bozell, *McCarthy and His Enemies: The Record and Its Meaning*, Prologue by William Schlamm. Chicago: Henry Regnery Co., 1954.

Burlingame, Roger, *Don't Let Them Scare You: The Life and Times of Elmer Davis*. Philadelphia: J. B. Lippincott Co., 1961.

———, *March of the Iron Men*. New York: Charles Scribner's Sons, 1938.

———, *Peace Veterans*. New York: Minton, Balch & Co., 1932.

Cain, Edward R., "The Legion Invades a Campus" in *The Nation*, Sept. 9, 1961.

Carr, Robert K., *The House Committee on Un-American Activities, 1945–1950*. Ithaca, N.Y.: Cornell University Press, 1952.

239

Chafee, Zechariah, *The Blessings of Liberty*. Philadelphia: J. R. Lippincott Co., 1956.

Chamberlain, Lawrence H., *Loyalty and Legislative Action*. Ithaca, N.Y.: Cornell University Press, 1951.

Chaplin, Ralph, *The Centralia Conspiracy*. Chicago: General Defense Committee, 1924.

Churchill, Winston S., *The Gathering Storm*. Boston: Houghton Mifflin Co., 1948.

——, Speech delivered at Westminster College, Fulton, Mo., Mar. 4, 1946.

Comfort, Mildred Houghton, *J. Edgar Hoover, Modern Knight Errant*. Minneapolis: T. S. Denison & Co., 1959.

Cooke, Alistair, *A Generation on Trial*. New York: Alfred A. Knopf, 1950.

Davis, Elmer, *But We Were Born Free*. Indianapolis: The Bobbs-Merrill Co., 1954.

Deane, John R., *The Strange Alliance: The Story of Our Efforts at Wartime Co-operation with Russia*. New York: The Viking Press, 1947.

Dilling, Elizabeth, *The Red Network: A "Who's Who" and Handbook of Radicalism for Patriots*. Chicago: Published by the author, 1934.

Donner, Frank J., *The Un-Americans*. New York: Ballantine Books, 1961.

Du Bois, W. E. B., *Dusk of Dawn*. New York: Harcourt, Brace & Co., 1940.

Duffield, Marcus, *King Legion*. New York: Jonathan Cape and Harrison Smith, 1931.

Faulkner, Harold Underwood, *The Quest for Social Justice, 1898–1914*, New York: The Macmillan Co., 1931.

Frankfurter, Felix, *The Case of Sacco and Vanzetti: A Critical Analysis for Lawyers and Laymen*. Boston: Little, Brown & Co., 1927.

Freedom to Read Bulletin. New York: American Book Publishers Council, Inc., 1962.

Gardiner, Alfred George, *Portraits and Portents*. New York: Harper & Brothers, 1926.

Gellermann, William, *The American Legion as Educator*. New York: Bureau of Publications, Teachers College, Columbia University, 1938.

——, *Martin Dies*, New York: John Day Co., 1944.

Gellhorn, Walter, *Individual Freedom and Governmental Restraints*. Baton Rouge, La.: Louisiana State University Press, 1956.

——, *Security, Loyalty, and Science*. Ithaca, N.Y.: Cornell University Press, 1950.

Gillmor, Dan, *Fear, the Accuser*. New York: Abelard-Schuman, Ltd., 1954.

Gray, Justin, with Victor H. Bernstein, *The Inside Story of the Legion*. New York: Boni & Gaer, 1948.

Grodzins, Morton, *The Loyal and the Disloyal*. Chicago: University of Chicago Press, 1956.

Haines, C. Grove, and Ross J. S. Hoffman, *The Origins and Background of the Second World War*. New York: Oxford University Press, 1947.

Hapgood, Norman (ed.), *Professional Patriots*. New York: Albert and Charles Boni, 1927.

Hart, Hornell, *McCarthy versus the State Department*. Durham, N.C.: Privately printed, 1952.

Hays, Arthur G., *Trial by Prejudice*. New York: Covici, Friede, 1933.

Henry, John J., *Campaign against Quebec*. Watertown, N.Y.: Knowlton and Rice, 1844.

Hoover, J. Edgar, *Masters of Deceit*. New York: Henry Holt & Co., 1958.

——, *Persons in Hiding*, Foreword by Courtney Ryley Cooper. Boston: Little, Brown & Co., 1938.

Johnson James, *Negro Americans, What Now?* New York: The Viking Press, 1934.

Joughin, George Louis, and Edmund M. Morgan, *The Legacy of Sacco and Vanzetti*. New York: Harcourt, Brace and Co., 1948.

Kennan, George F., *Russia Leaves the War*. Princeton, N.J.: Princeton University Press, 1956.

——, *Russia and the West under Lenin and Stalin*. Boston: Little, Brown & Co., 1961.

Kennedy, John F., "College Loyalty Oaths" in *Coronet*, April, 1960.

Konvitz, Milton R., *Fundamental Liberties of a Free People*. Ithaca, N.Y.: Cornell University Press, 1957.

241

Lane, Winthrop D., "The Buford Widows" in *The Survey,* Jan. 10, 1920.

Lattimore, Owen, *Ordeal by Slander.* Boston: Little, Brown & Co., 1950.

Lederer, William J., *A Nation of Sheep.* New York: W. W. Norton Co., 1961.

Lowenthal, Max, *The Federal Bureau of Investigation.* New York: William Sloane Associates, Inc., 1950.

McCarthy, Joseph R., *Retreat from Victory: The Story of George C. Marshall.* Privately printed, 1952.

Maslow, Will, "Case History of a Smear" in *Congress Weekly* (American Jewish Congress), Oct. 19, 1953.

Miller, Merle, *The Judges and the Judged,* Foreword by Robert E. Sherwood. New York: Doubleday & Co., 1952.

Minutes of a Communist Cell on Art. Fullerton, Calif.: Educational News Service, 1960.

Morison, Samuel E., and Henry S. Commager, *The Growth of the American Republic.* In 2 vols.; New York: Oxford University Press, 1937.

Mosk, Stanley, and Howard H. Jewel, "The Birch Phenomenon Analyzed" in *The New York Times Magazine,* Aug. 20, 1961.

Murray, Robert K., "Alexander Mitchell Palmer" in *Dictionary of American Biography.* New York: Charles Scribner's Sons, 1928–1958. XXII (Supplement Two) 510.

————, *Red Scare: A Study in National Hysteria.* Minneapolis: University of Minnesota Press, 1955.

Myrdal, Gunnar, *An American Dilemma.* New York: Harper & Brothers, 1944.

Nolan, William A., *Communsim versus the Negro.* Chicago: Henry Regnery Co., 1951.

Ogden, August R., *The Dies Committee.* Washington: Catholic University of America Press, 1945.

Pierce, Bessie Louise, *Public Opinion and the Teaching of History in the United States.* New York: Alfred A. Knopf, 1926.

Record, Wilson, *The Negro and the Communist Party.* Chapel Hill, N.C.: University of North Carolina Press, 1951.

"Red Channels: The Report of Communist Influence in Radio and Television," in *Counterattack, the Newsletter of Facts to Combat Communism,* 1950.

Rovere, Richard H., *Senator Joe McCarthy*. New York: Harcourt, Brace and Co., 1959.

Rowse, Alfred Leslie, *Appeasement: A Study in Political Decline*. New York: W. W. Norton Co., 1961.

Sawyer, Charles W., *Firearms in American History, 1600–1800*. Boston: Published by the author, 1910.

Shannon, David, "William English Walling" in *Dictionary of American Biography*, Supplement Two. New York: Charles Scribner's Sons, 1928–1958, XXII, 290.

Shirer, William L., *The Rise and Fall of the Third Reich*. New York: Simon & Schuster, 1960.

Smith, Alfred E., Public Papers of Governor Smith. Albany: 1920.

Stevenson, Adlai E., "America under Pressure" in *Harper's Magazine*, August, 1961.

Taylor, Telford, *Grand Inquest: The Story of Congressional Investigations*, Ballantine Edition. New York: Ballantine Books, 1961.

Trotsky, Leon, *Lenin*. Garden City, New York: Garden City Books, 1959.

Wechsler, James, *The Age of Suspicion*. New York: Random House, 1953.

Welch, Robert, *Blue Book of the John Birch Society*. Published by the Society, 1958.

Werner, Arthur, "The Truth about the American Legion" in *The Nation*, July 6 and 13, 1921.

Wheeler-Bennett, John W., *The Forgotten Peace: Brest-Litovsk, March, 1918*. New York: William Morrow & Co., 1939.

Wiggins, James Russell, *Freedom or Secrecy?* New York: Oxford University Press, 1956.

Wynn, Daniel Webster, *The NAACP versus Negro Revolutionary Protest: A Comparative Study of the Effectiveness of Each Movement*. New York: Exposition Press, 1955.

DOCUMENTARY MATERIAL

Attorney General. Annual Reports, 1909, 1919.

Bills to Curb or Outlaw the Communist Party of the United States. Hearings before House Committee on Un-American Activities. 80th Congress, 1st Session, March, 1947.

Brewing and Liquor Interests and German and Bolshevik Propaganda. Report of a Subcommittee of the Senate Committee on the Judiciary. Sen. Doc. No. 61, 66th Congress, 1st Session, 1919.

Communism in the District of Columbia. Hearings before House Committee on Un-American Activities, July, 1949.

Communism in Labor Unions in the United States. Hearings before House Committee on Un-American Activities, 1947.

Communist Espionage in the United States Government. Hearings before House Committee on Un-American Activities, July, August, September, 1948.

Communist Infiltration of Minority Groups. Hearings before House Committee on Un-American Activities, July, 1949.

Communist Infiltration of the Motion Picture Industry. Hearings before House Committee on Un-American Activities, October, 1947.

Communist Training Operations. Hearings before House Committee on Un-American Activities, 1960.

Congressional Record. Designated CR in footnotes. For example, 100 CR 1472 means volume 100, page 1472. CRA means CR Appendix.

House Report No. 2618, 83d Congress, 2d Session, Aug. 4, 1954 (Testimony of Dr. James Killian, p. 37).

Institute of Pacific Relations. Hearings before Internal Security Subcommittee of Senate Committee on Judiciary, 1952.

Interlocking Subversion in Government Departments. Hearings before Internal Security Subcommittee of Senate Committee on Judiciary. 83d Congress, 1st Session, 1953.

Investigation of Un-American Activities in the United States. Hearings on resolution to establish Special (Dies) House Committee and testimony on German-American Bund. 75th Congress, 3d Session, August, 1938.

New York State Journal, 159th Session, 1936, I, 56–63 (McNaboe Resolution).

Nuremberg Documents. A portion of these has been published in the United States in *Nazi Conspiracy and Aggression,* 10 vols. (1946), and *Trials of War Criminals before the Nuremberg Military Tribunals,* 15 vols. (1951–52); Washington: Government Printing Office.

Preliminary Report on Totalitarian Propaganda in the United States. Part III of Appendix to *Investigation of Un-American Activities in the United States.* Hearings before Special (Dies) Committee on Un-American Activities in House of Representatives, 1941.

Radical Right: A Fact Sheet, The. Prepared by Commission on Law and Social Action of the American Jewish Congress. New York, 1961.

Report of Joint Legislative Committee of the State of New York Investigating Seditious Activities. Albany, 1920.

Report on John Birch Society to Governor Edmund D. Brown of California by Stanley Mosk, Attorney-General, and Howward H. Jewel, Assistant Attorney-General of California, July 7, 1961.

Report upon the Illegal Practices of the United States Department of Justice. By 12 American lawyers. Washington: National Popular Government League, 1920.

Soviet Espionage within the United States Government. Second Report of House Committee on Un-American Activities. Dec. 31, 1948.

State Department Employee Loyalty Investigation. Report of Committee on Foreign Relations (Senate Report No. 2108). 81st Congress, 2d Session, 1950.

Index